THE FIVE

Business

Little ^ Pigs

Helping Reluctant Business Owners build simple profitable businesses they love.

TAMARA SIMON

First published in 2016 by Business Scene Investigation
Wavell Heights
Brisbane, Australia
thebsi.com.au

National Library of Australia Cataloguing-in-Publication entry
Author: Tamara Simon
The Five Little Business Pigs: Helping Reluctant Business Owners build simple profitable businesses they love
ISBN: 9780994577504
Subject: Business – Small Business
Dewey Number: 658.022

Book cover: pipelinedesign.com.au
Publishing services: pipelinedesign.com.au
Print: paradigmprintmedia.com.au

Disclaimer

The material in this publication is of the nature of general comment only, and does not represent professional advice. It is not intended to provide specific guidance for particular circumstances and it should not be relied on as the basis of any decision to take action or not take action on any matter it covers. Readers should obtain professional advice where appropriate, before making any such decision. To the maximum extent permitted by law, the author and publisher disclaim all responsibility and liability to any person, arising directly or indirectly from any person taking or not taking action based on the information in this publication.

For Mum and Dad

*Words can't express my gratitude for everything
your love, support and guidance has given me.*

I am the person I am because of both of you.

For Mark

*Without your enduring love, support and encouragement,
this book would never have been written.*

Contents

Acknowledgements

*A true relationship is someone who accepts
your past, supports your present, loves you
unconditionally and encourages your future.*

Unknown

There are so many people to thank who helped bring the idea of a book into reality.

Firstly, and most importantly, I'd like to thank Mark, Mum and Dad for their love, encouragement and support. They've been on the sidelines, cheering me on, ever since I embarked on this crazy, frustrating, overwhelming and fulfilling journey; at times wondering, 'How long does it take to write The Book?' Hopefully, they are now very proud of the result and of having a published author in their midst.

I'd like to thank Andrew Griffiths, Key Person of Influence's (KPI) publishing mentor and #1 small business author, for providing the framework to write this book and encouraging me to strike out in a different direction when, what I thought was my only idea, lost traction.

I'd like to thank the amazing members of The Collective – Brenda, Helen, Jason, Natalia, Phill and Will – who've pushed me along when times have been tough and have always had faith that I would do this, even when I doubted myself.

In particular, I owe a great deal of gratitude to Brenda Jamnik, who read the whole book and spent hours editing and reworking my concepts and writing so I could hand my editor a book in much better shape than the first draft. Brenda also kept me accountable and gave me the confidence to keep writing rather than shelving it; this book could not have been written without her invaluable input and support.

Thanks also to Elizabeth Camillo, my new interstate and Skype Accountability Buddy who quickly read the book and provided great feedback.

To my Mastermind Group: Julie, Jennie, Natasha and Tanja. I know it's taken a long time to see the outcome, but thanks so much for your support and your ideas of when and how to take my business to the next level. Huge thanks also to Jules for opening up new opportunities for me, as well as writing the foreword and helping me realise this result.

I'd like to thank Peter Reardon who designed the the book cover, my BPS Roadmap model and brought my Pigs idea to life.

I'd like to thank everyone who said, 'That's a great idea for a book.' It kept me going when the words weren't always flowing.

I'd like to thank my clients, the businesses I've worked with and the people I've met thus far whose experiences and ideas have been woven into these pages.

And I'd like to thank you, my readers, who have contributed to helping find a cure to fight dementia by purchasing this book. I hope my book gives you the ideas and strategies to build an even better business that is simple, profitable and one you love.

All the best

Tamara

Foreword

From Surviving to Thriving

I don't know about you but my business story wasn't derived from a burning desire to be a business owner nor from a ground breaking idea or product that would change the world.

It evolved from unforeseen circumstances and a primal maternal instinct to provide for my children.

At 35 years of age, I found myself divorced with two young children to support and no idea of how I would do that with no money and no job.

Thankfully my brother, who had a successful financial planning business, offered me an admin position at $25.25 per hour, and an opportunity to learn a new career and make a change in my life. So my life encompassed a tiny 2 bedroom house for my children and I, and a massive desire to earn enough income to survive.

Looking back, this was <u>the</u> moment of change.

Three years down the track, I was faced with another challenge. My brother retired and I was forced to decide 'Do I stay in survival mode and work for someone else or do I step forward, make a change and create my own business?'

My brother's comments, which helped me make the decision, still stay in my mind: 'Haven't I taught you anything these past three years? You know everything about this business, how it works from the ground up. Now is your time to go out and be your own boss.'

Lucky for me, I was given my first client and embarked on a whole new world of being a Business Owner. The notion of having your own business sounds wonderful, exciting and full of shiny things; but the reality was I was still in survival mode, working 7 days a week to meet the workload and trying to balance my personal life with my children.

This ultimately led to pure physical exhaustion and being fully overwhelmed by stress. This was my moment of realising: 'Do I stay in survival mode or do I spend time building systems in my business to move forward?' I realised I had all the knowledge in my head and no solid foundations to grow (and this is why you need to read this book).

After many tears and glasses of wine as well as amazing support and reality chats with my partner and surrounding myself with likeminded business friends, I realised three things:

1. I didn't know the numbers of my business which is not viable.

2. I was doing everything myself – I had no systems, I had very little written down – just my own bits of paper and notes to remind myself to do this and do that. And no one could make sense of it, let alone follow it. I needed strong practical procedures and processes in place to move away from the survival mode and into a business that is self-sustaining and profitable.

3. The only way out was to duplicate myself and to build solid business foundations so someone could then help me with the work.

So I took the plunge and employed someone who could write simple processes. They followed me around, wrote down everything I said and did and turned that into procedures and systems which I then checked and tweaked. After 12 months of steadily doing this whilst I was still doing client work which paid the bills and supported my family, I had documented systems in place and built up solid foundations around my business model. This led to me surrounding myself with capable staff and gaining a firm profitable business model which can be replicated.

Specialist PMC, over the last year, has grown to having 8 amazing staff members and an extremely profitable business process and management plan.

But ... I've only been able to have this success and growth because I understand and know my numbers which I track every day, and I invested time and money in documenting great systems in my business.

I met Tamara 12 months ago when I joined an Elite Masterminding Group and she has helped me enormously with understanding how I need strong firm foundations, processes and a management plan to move me through all phases of my business growth which I wish to achieve. Her supportive advice and understanding has created a massive change in how I view my business, the management of my staff and my business moving forward.

Tamara has been the Troubleshooter and sounding board for my business.

I recommend this book to anyone who wants to move from being The Reluctant Business Owner (which was me) to someone who loves and understands all facets of their business so they can do the work they love, get help for the things they don't, and truly have the lifestyle business which gives them the financial freedom they desired.

Julie Tasker – Owner and Managing Director
Specialist PMC
www.specialistpmc.com.au

PS The success of this business makes me grateful for the life I have and the financial freedom it has given me, so a big shout out to my brother for being an amazing Business Mentor.

Introduction

Time is such a precious commodity and to think people are making a choice to read my book rather than doing something else (or reading someone else's book), well, I'm very grateful.

I assure you that your time will be an investment in further understanding the intricacies of your business as well as providing guidance on how to confront challenges and turn them into opportunities by finding simple solutions.

Without knowing you personally, I wonder what prompted you to pick up my book and say, 'That's for me.'

- The title intrigued you and you wanted to find out more.

- You liked the fairytale 'The Three Little Pigs' as a child and wanted to see my take on things.

- You want to change how you're running your business and are looking for different ideas.

- You have just started your business or are about to grow your business, and you want some tips and tricks to help you on your journey.

- You were about to get on a plane and thought this book looked more interesting than what was otherwise on offer.

Whatever the reason (and I'd love you to share that with me by dropping me an email via my website), again thanks. I'm constantly looking for different ways to improve the way I operate my business, and I'm keen to learn from those who have done it before and can discuss the successes and challenges which had to be managed.

This book has been designed and written for anyone who wants to build an even better business, and I think (and hope) that includes everyone who owns or is the key leader in the business.

As all business owners know from experience, running a business is hard. If you're doing everything solo which includes many of us when we first start out, it can not only be hard but also very lonely. At times you may feel that it's you against the world.

Having been through this solo journey and experiencing those feelings on and off since I started my business in 2002, I decided to write this book. It was not only a way of giving my crazy ideas life, but I also hoped to provide others in a similar situation with something of value; food for thought that could possibly help every business owner out there, large or small, deal with their challenges.

No matter what type of business you're currently running or want to run, I know from experience every business should be three things:

1. Simple

2. Profitable

3. One you love

Simple does not mean cheap and it doesn't mean dumbing things down to the nth degree.

Simple is not jargon but can be lots of visuals and as few words as possible, explaining how things are done.

Simple means everyone is clear on what your business is about: what you do and how you do it.

Simple is about everyone, be it primarily one person or a team of twenty, being clear on how their part makes things happen.

Does this sound good to you? Great.

Let's start this journey together and I will show you how the fairytale 'The Three Little Pigs' was really about building simple, profitable businesses.

Part One

The Five Little Business Pigs

What do you need to start a business?
Three simple things:
know your product better than anyone else,
know your customer and
have a burning desire to succeed.

Dave Thomas

Chapter 1

The Reluctant Business Owner

Living in continual chaos is exhausting and frightening.
The catch is that is also very addictive.

Lorna Luft

There are so many hats a business owner has to wear. Which one are you wearing now? Do I hear you say 'only one' because I'm juggling six at the moment? You could be spending your days in many different ways:

- Chasing your tail
- Rushing from one place to another
- Dealing with never-ending emails
- Switching from task to task
- Bouncing from client to client
- On the phone, wondering if this is the best use of your time

- Doing a lot but feeling like you're getting absolutely nowhere

If so, welcome to the life of a business owner, the side nobody told you about or if they did, you thought they were exaggerating because they seemed to have it all.

The above list comes from comments I have heard many small business owners make, people who know how tough it sometimes gets trying to juggle too many things (business, clients, work, family and friends) while wearing those many but necessary hats.

Let me ask again, how many hats are you *really* wearing? How many of the following apply?

1. Networker
2. Business Developer
3. Salesperson
4. Decision maker
5. Marketer
6. Bookkeeper/Payroll Officer/Accountant
7. Receptionist
8. Human Resources
9. Change Manager
10. Partnerships
11. Strategist
12. Writer/Product developer
13. Counsellor/Supporter
14. Administration
15. Trainer
16. Cleaner

Feel free to add others to get your final number:

_____

_____

_____

_____

What magical number did you finish with: ten, twelve, fourteen, twenty-two?

Whatever the number is, it's probably higher than you thought it would be.

How often do you feel like you're living to work rather than working to live? Are you juggling so many things and wearing many different hats just to keep your business surviving when you aspire to have it thriving?

The good news is you're not alone. You will see, as I outline the journey of a small business owner, that I'm walking right there with you in those sometimes heavy, sometimes light shoes. And the even better news, which you will realise as you read this book, is your business journey doesn't have to remain like this.

If you are like most small business owners, your business evolved from one of four sets of circumstances. Which one prompted you?

1. As a technician or expert in a particular area, you decided to utilise your experience to educate others, and hopefully more make money doing it.

2. You had a great idea, story or experience which translated into a need or passion to pursue that avenue instead of remaining at your existing job.

3. You were in a job where you could see how the boss did things and decided you didn't want to be there anymore because you thought you could handle things in a better way.

4. It all began by fluke or accident (which some might call good luck).

Many small business owners don't have a driving passion to run their business and all that comes with it. Instead, what they do have is passion and technical expertise in a particular area or industry sector. It is this skill they wish to impart to others whilst also wanting to make a difference by helping people.

I fell into running and owning a business. It wasn't something I'd ever thought of doing and it wasn't even on the radar as I started down my career path. But what I found as I moved from one job to another (generally after eighteen months to the day) was that I liked variety and learning new things. I realised if I couldn't move up in the organisation, I would rather move on because I got bored and wanted something new.

The reasons I established my own business included that I had achieved leadership and management success relatively early in my working life, I was working very long hours and I had gained a great reputation for being able to get things sorted efficiently and quickly.

I knew (or thought I knew) how to operate a business, having run a not-for-profit for the previous two years, and I was keen to devote the long hardworking hours for my own benefit rather than someone else's. In October 2002, I had an opportunity to leverage my skills so I became a business owner. With my reputation as a Troubleshooter, the confidence I had gained from being a Queensland finalist in the Telstra Business Awards and a few contacts, I was ready to give it a go.

If I'm really honest, my business also arose from a need for self-preservation brought about by continued frustration. Why? On more than one occasion, I had been deemed a threat to management and staff rather than being valued as a bright, energetic young individual who completed things quicker than most. I was willing to put in the necessary time and effort to achieve an organisation's outcomes while simultaneously helping whomever I could along the way.

Unfortunately, the value of my experience and skills was not acknowledged, in the form of either praise or an increased pay packet. After this had gone on for too long, I decided it was time to move on. And I am so grateful I had the courage to take this step.

It started with a great idea

Why do so many businesses start out as angels and then, out of nowhere it seems, turn into devils that their owners curse and sometimes feel chained to?

The cycle of small businesses usually starts with someone deciding to leave paid work to set up their own business to gain the freedom and lifestyle they desire; to make money; and to do whatever they are passionate about – whether that's as a mobile hairdresser, consultant, accountant, bookkeeper, trainer or product developer.

If you are one of those of who has been brave enough to set up your own business, I'm sure there have been times when you've asked yourself, 'Why did I do this?' But you persist because you are passionate about what you do and this is why you're in business in the first place.

Perhaps, like most business owners, you started with a great idea that allowed you to actually open the business. And you were excited when that first client paid. Your first client, *woo-hoo*, and you were on our way.

A business often starts off great, with lots of enthusiasm. Then there are the unusually long hours to bring business in the door because primarily it's all about getting money in the bank to pay the bills, keep the house and look after yourself and your family. You don't mind the long hours because you're just starting out. It won't be like this for long, you tell yourself and others, to justify why you keep missing dinner or nights out with friends.

Your reputation grows, partly by word of mouth, and the business starts to get busier. You have more and more work, leading to even longer hours – but hopefully more money.

Work then increases to a point where you decide to take on a team member to help you, but this also creates more work and all of a sudden the business now has a team of five then ten then twenty; and you, the business owner, are spending all your time dealing with mistakes, rework, staff issues, complaints and troubleshooting whilst working hard to get new clients in the door.

If this sounds like you and your journey, maybe one or more of the following applies:

- You're working harder than when you first started but it's not reflected in your bottom line or your bank account.

- You're working harder and harder just to pay for the lifestyles and lives of your employees, but sacrificing your own.

- You're spending all day chasing your tail.

- You can see and feel your team doing a lot of work but it's stressful: things don't seem to be going well and you don't know why.

If these points resonate with you, it's possible that as part of your success, you're saying *yes* to everything and everyone: For example, yes you can train in anything; yes you can do social media; yes you can market to any industry sector; yes you can build high rise commercial developments and not just low set homes; yes you can attend another unproductive meeting; yes you can induct a new staff member; and yes you can be on call 24/7.

Even if you know nothing about a task or have no experience in an industry area, you believe you can do it all. You'll find the people you need (you say this but often don't) or do it yourself (the usual option) but either way, you say you will make it happen because this is what business owners do when they start a business. They agree to everything because their only focus is getting the job done to get money in the bank which, funnily enough, is very important.

Why does this consistently happen? Why is this the norm rather than the exception in how people start their businesses?

If you were building a house, you wouldn't do it like this. You wouldn't approach the project reactively. You wouldn't find a block of land and exclaim, 'Let's start building,' and then commence putting down a slab made of uneven concrete, stick or brick.

You would put plans in place. You would find the best people for the job according to your budget. You may even have someone to manage the process so you can focus on what you do best. You would then find a block of land and put down the foundations. You would consider how many rooms you wanted: how many garages; where the bedrooms would be and whether they would be all together, with the kids' bedrooms near Mum and Dad; whether there was going to be a media room; what the design of the kitchen would be like etc.

A lot of thought goes into the building of a house and business owners should work through the same process. Questions to ask yourself include:

- What specific services am I offering rather than just whingeing about the work I'm doing (and the stuff I never, ever wanted to do)?

- What do I really want to do (that people will part with their cash for)?

- What am I really good at?

- What work am I not good at or prefer not to do, and how can I find people to help with these tasks?

You may be reading this and thinking, well I did all that. If so, I commend you and offer my congratulations. However, many business owners not only struggle with developing the key focus for their business i.e. the business model, products, services, pricing structure etc. which is then reflected in their Annual Business Plan; but they also struggle with what is commonly called either 'The Pitch' or 'The Elevator Speech'. Instead of explaining quickly, succinctly and simply that they help specific clients with specific problems which they will solve with specific services, they use lots of convoluted words that don't say much at all. They try to be everything to everyone and end up not knowing exactly who they will help or why because they lack clarity and simplicity. This makes it very difficult for me to refer them to a potential client. After all, if I can't work out what they do and articulate it in their absence, how can anyone else?

But until you nail your key focus and your pitch, your business will stagnate and you will continue to do work you don't want to do, for clients you don't want to work with, for money that doesn't truly represent your knowledge, experience and value.

To understand this more fully or to see a different perspective on pitching, I encourage you to watch the TV shows *The Pitch*, *Dragon's Den* and the Australian spin-off *Shark Tank*. Basically, the clarity of your Pitch will result in the type of business you have and the outcomes you gain, which will result in your ultimate success (or lack thereof). As has been said by Daniel Priestley, author of *Key Person of Influence*, 'You only get what you pitch for and you're always pitching'.

What should I do?

By now, you may be feeling worn out, frustrated and tired of running your business. These are all symptoms that something isn't quite right, so there is now a decision to make.

But before you ponder that decision, stop for a moment, take a breath and realise what an amazing individual you are. If clients are still coming through the door and money is in the bank (even if only fleetingly), you must be doing something right.

And also acknowledge the fantastic leadership decision (the first of many A-ha moments to come as you read on) you have just made for your business. You've recognised there are some issues to consider, and you've decided you don't want to continue being the mouse on the treadmill; running around aimlessly, wasting time, money and energy and getting nowhere. It's your choice.

Remember: Not all business owners reach the point where they recognise that something has to change, even if they don't quite know what that is yet. Understanding that it's time to do things differently is a crucial first step to building a profitable business you love.

The next step is to draw a line in the sand and say to yourself: *This can't continue and I'm going to start changing today.*

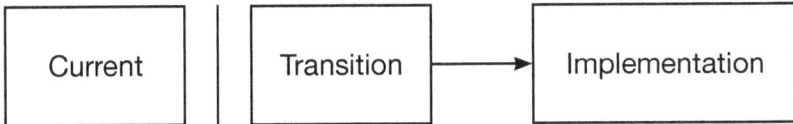

```
┌──────────┐  ┌──────────┐          ┌──────────────┐
│          │  │          │          │              │
│ Current  │  │Transition│ ───────▶ │Implementation│
│          │  │          │          │              │
└──────────┘  └──────────┘          └──────────────┘
```

You wouldn't build a house like this

To return to the house example, before beginning construction on a new home, your detailed building plans would probably include many items:

- The overall look (goal and outcome) of the house

- Measurements for all rooms

- Materials and equipment required for all components

- Timeframes for completion of everything

- Suppliers selected to deliver the required outcomes for the build

- Steps to be completed in numerical order, taking into account those which could happen simultaneously.

- Contingency options for when things don't go as planned such as too many wet weather days, poor workmanship, budget blowouts and other risk mitigation strategies.

- Budget and costs required upfront before construction can begin and then throughout construction, as well as costs required for regular maintenance.

It would be logical to outline all these things first, not only to ensure you build the house you desire, but also that you also have the money and skills to complete the job.

If you agree it's essential to lay down strong and solid foundations when a house is built to ensure it stands the tests of time, why would you build a business without laying similar strong solid foundations?

Common reasons people give for skipping these steps:

- They feel time poor

- They have no time for planning

- They had a plan but discarded it quickly when things were changed (often for the worse)

- They believe it's a waste of time because the market changes too quickly

- They are not clear where to start

- They are new to the process and lack the necessary business acumen (they don't know what they don't know)

These reasons all indicate there's very little value being placed on planning. And I consider each one invalid. Why? Because I know no one would build a house under these conditions.

I recommend you think about re-building your business as though you were building a house. What do you think – no, let me rephrase that – what do you *know* you would do?

You'd talk to people who have built houses before and ask, 'What did you learn?' and 'How much did it cost?' You'd work out whether you want a brick or timber house, or a Queenslander style or modern contemporary home. You would find a designer to design the intricacies of your house (because you have to adhere to so many rules and building codes). You would also find a builder because you're probably not an expert in this field (that of building a house), and you want it to last the distance and maybe re-sell down the track.

I would hazard a guess you have rarely applied these same principles to your business. Perhaps it's time to change how you view your business so you can move from your current model to one that's more sustainable, simple, profitable and one you actually love.

Once you begin thinking about building your business in the same way as a house, one of the most important things to remember is the key to success is developing systems using *who, what, when, where, how* and *why* questions to determine the detail.

However, systems (which are more than your policies and procedures, IT or your files) are not the only component required to build a simple profitable business you love. There are three key components, of which systems are only one; and all three should be considered, evaluated and in balance. I describe this balance and concept as the Business, People and Systems (BPS) triangle.

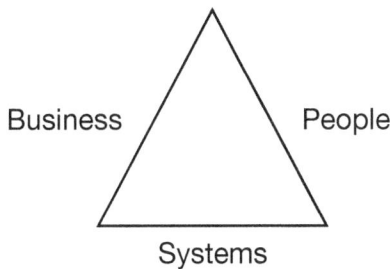

Business   People

Systems

It's important to understand the details of how your business operates as well as what your people are doing. Successful profitable businesses, even those operating as solo businesses, all have great people helping them, inside and out. Why? Because no one can achieve success on their own.

Are you tapping into the best people to help take you and your business forward? Or are you still isolated, doing your best to achieve everything on your own because you believe or have heard that if you ask for help, you have failed. Maybe you just don't have the money to bring in the necessary expertise and help?

If you truly believe this, please put my book down now and read any autobiography by any successful business person – Richard Branson, Steve Jobs, Janine Allis – to see how this thinking is not only incorrect but limiting to you and your business potential. And until you have shifted and are in this positive mindset, I can't help you any further.

Now you have done that or are already in the right mindset, please keep reading.

The Systems part of the triangle is all about solid foundations and stability, for now and into the future. Your business may not have good systems in place at the moment, but after reading this book, you will understand what the word *systems* actually means and that they are the critical piece in the puzzle which tie everything together. So read on: more information and the solutions are coming.

Many business owners understand they need policies and procedures as part of their operations, but they rarely invest the time and money to document how those operations work. This means all this knowledge remains in the head of the business owner, and as the business grows, in the heads of their team members. And if this knowledge isn't documented, years of experience can walk out the door, leaving a dysfunctional business with dysfunctional operations.

Perhaps you are the rare business owner who does have documented policies and procedures. Could you improve them? Have you reviewed them recently and are they consistently updated? Could you make the processes simpler and quicker without compromising quality and consistency for your clients?

By now I hope you can see that systems (your solid foundations) are the key to any business: you *must* have solid foundations. And just like when you build a house, you must lay down good foundations before you even start because you can't put the roof on first.

Embrace the title

Have you truly embraced the title of 'Business Owner' or are you what I affectionately term the 'Reluctant Business Owner'? Does the title 'Business Owner' or maybe even the word 'reluctant' make you recoil? Are you wishing I would change topics because I'm hitting too close to home?

Being the Reluctant Business Owner is not a bad term or one to shy away from. It's the modus operandi of numerous small to medium business owners who may have started out loving what they did but now find the joy has been quashed by the realities of running a business. It is clear to me that many people are wearing the Reluctant Business Owner uniform.

What exactly does the term 'Reluctant Business Owner' mean and how did it come about?

Many business owners are reluctant to embrace everything encompassed in the title 'Business Owner' because they prefer spending their time doing the fun stuff, the work that gives them energy and makes them feel good about themselves. They would rather be onsite with clients than completing mandatory business processes; thinking about sales, marketing, writing procedures, accounts and other necessary administrative tasks. (Personally, I would rather be speaking, facilitating and problem solving.) And because they don't enjoy it, they either ignore it; thinking it will all get better or go away, or procrastinate to the point that it doesn't get done at all.

Here's the seven main phrases the Reluctant Business Owner will use:

1. **I'm too busy to ...** tell people (including myself) that I'm too busy to write the annual business plan or amend it as you go along; define my products and services so I don't become everything to everyone; document what's in my head about how my business works so I can delegate, have a holiday, get some help, and ultimately have a scalable and saleable business.

2. **There's just me so I don't need to ...** document anything in a way that anyone else needs to follow; write a plan that's clear and concise about what needs to be done and by when; have a tidy office or desk especially since I work from home.

3. **I'm not good at ...** sales, marketing or finance; in fact, anything that's not the fun or energising stuff for you. (This usually means these things are being avoided or not done very well.)

4. **Turnover's great but I've got little or no cash ...** (This phrase is based on owners letting themselves get caught up in the turnover hype rather than knowing their numbers inside out to ensure they are making a profit. Just because there is money in the bank doesn't mean the business is being run profitably.)

5. **I don't want to know ...** anything bad about my business, clients or market because if I ignore it or bury my head in the sand for long enough, it will either go away or get better. (Unfortunately, wishing it doesn't make it so).

6. **Do I have to ...** look at my numbers or accounts; phone potential clients; do admin, engage on social media, write anything down when I'm busy just doing the critical stuff like completing paid work?

7. **Why can't everyone just leave me alone so I can get my work done?** (This includes clients, staff, phone calls, endless meetings, emails etc.)

These seven phases of thought lead to the ultimate phrase and sign of the Reluctant Business Owner: *It's all good, no worries.* Meaning: My head is in the sand and I hope that if I stay there long enough, things will either get better or go away all by themselves. (I have to tell you that neither of these things will happen.)

If you're thinking or saying any of these phrases, I'm sorry to say you are the Reluctant Business Owner which means it's time to leave the fairytale behind and face reality.

Albert Einstein is attributed with the saying: 'The definition of insanity is doing the same thing over and over again but expecting different results.' The overarching theme of all Reluctant Business Owners is they keep employing the same strategy (albeit often unconsciously) while making the same mistakes and ending up in the same financial position year after year. Why? Because they haven't stopped to actually learn this lesson and do something differently.

If you identify yourself as the Reluctant Business Owner, I'm sure that from time to time you have felt and said at least one of the seven phrases since commencing your business. I know I have.

> Learn the Lesson

And that's okay. But if you truly want to be a successful business owner and take your business to the next level, you must fully embrace what this really means. A true business owner is identified by their actions and not a meaningless title.

I have written this book for all those Reluctant Business Owners who started out with the dream of owning a business that would provide them with financial freedom, a lifestyle of their choosing and flexibility, but who now need help to get their business back on track. Without embracing the good, bad and ugly of being a business owner and all the tasks, stress and fun that comes with it, all you really have is a job. And isn't that what you thought you'd escaped?

If you want to build a simple profitable business you actually love, I encourage you to keep reading. The time to change starts now and it all starts with *you*.

The Three Little Pigs

Before I begin my discussion of the Five Little Business Pigs, I would like to give you a different spin on the original fairytale, as told by Kermit the Frog from a 'Sesame Street News' segment, found at bit.ly/1W6UqcL. Kermit interviews each of the three Pigs after the Wolf has been and gone, asking them how they are feeling.

Straw Pig: *'Can I tell you about how I feel about that? What kind of a dumb question is that? I'm angry.'*

Stick Pig: *'How do I feel? How can you be so cruel as to ask me that when my house is in rubble? Sad, that's how I feel.'*

Brick Pig: *'I feel proud, yes proud. It took me a long time to build this house. It is the strongest house on the block and the old Wolf couldn't blow this down if he tried to. Yes I feel very, very proud.'*

At the end, the third little Pig (Brick) sees how upset the other two little Pigs are and says, *'Join me and Muffin for a little while,'* so it's a bit of a community effort in the end and everyone lives happily ever after. This is the rightful ending to any fairytale but unfortunately that's not always the case in real life.

What I love about 'The Three Little Pigs' fairytale and the Kermit the Frog video are the messages. In the video clip, the third little Pig (Brick) also says, *'Well, I had a vision. I took my time building this house of Bricks. It didn't happen overnight but I have pride in what I've done and I'm really happy with the result. There was quality in what I did and there was a reward at the end, and the reward was the house wasn't blown down at the end by the Wolf.'*

- There was a Vision
- There was Quality
- There was Pride
- There was a Reward

The third little Pig also made the decision to be a bit different which is what you must do with your business to be successful: play to your strengths and at the same time, be different from your competitors and add value to your clients.

The difference between who you are and who you want to be ... is what you do.

Unknown

You can dream the beautiful dream about having a business that's made of Brick but unless you put in enough time and effort, you will not achieve it. It will simply remain a Straw or Stick house because you want the reward of the business *without* falling in love with the process and effort needed to truly turn the dream into a wonderful and profitable reality.

⚲ Building your business .....
one brick at a time

Just as the third little Pig did, you need to build your business, one brick at a time. To help this process, at the end of each chapter I have posed three questions for you to consider.

These first three questions will show you how much you have (or have not) embraced your title as Business Owner:

1. **Do you have a one page annual business plan which clearly states your three key priorities for the year and how you will achieve them?**

2. **What is one thing you need to change to avoid being the Reluctant Business Owner?**

3. **When will you actually make this change?**

To help answer these questions, it might also be timely to review Charles Osgood's poem on responsibility to determine your current role as a business owner, and the role you would ultimately prefer to have.

Remember: *You* are responsible for making your business the very best.

THE RESPONSIBILITY POEM

There was a most important job that needed to be done,
And no reason not to do it, there was absolutely none.
But in vital matters such as this, the thing you have to ask
Is who exactly will it be who'll carry out the task?
Anybody could have told you that Everybody knew
That this was something Somebody would surely have to do.
Nobody was unwilling; Anybody had the ability.
But Nobody believed that it was their responsibility.
It seemed to be a job that Anybody could have done,
If Anybody thought they were supposed to be the one.
But since Everybody recognised that Anybody could,
Everybody took for granted that Somebody would.
But Nobody told Anybody that we are aware of,
That they would be in charge of seeing it was taken care of.
And Nobody took it on themselves to follow through,
And do what Everybody thought that Somebody would do.
When what Everybody needed did not get done at all,
Everybody was complaining that Somebody dropped the ball.
Anybody then could see it was an awful crying shame,
And Everybody looked around for Somebody to blame.
Somebody should have done the job
And Everybody should have.
But in the end Nobody did
What Anybody could have.

Charles Osgood

Now you have determined whether you are the Reluctant Business Owner and have been reminded of the messages in the fairytale, it's time for you to see inside my story and learn more about each house of The Five Little Business Pigs.

There is one more critical step to take, however, and that is to first consider that pesky Wolf bearing down on you, threatening to blow your business down at any moment.

Chapter 2

What are your Wolves?

You have to be so disciplined that even your distractions become focused.

Onyi Anyado

Remember the characteristics of the Wolf in the fairytale? Sneaky, appeared unexpectedly, cloaked in disguise. Does that sound like any of the distractions coming in and out of your business? What do you think the Wolves in your business might be?

Possibilities could be:

- You
- Your clients
- Your team
- Technology
- Something or someone else

Maybe you have more than one Wolf. To help you decide, let me share a story from my business journey.

I have worked in the vocational education and training (VET) sector for over twenty years. When I speak at conferences, I often ask the question: 'What is your Wolf?' Many registered training organisations (RTOs) immediately identify the Regulator as the Wolf in their business. But when I challenge them to dig a little deeper and reflect honestly on their business, they come to realise if they had truly built a Brick business, they would view the Regulator in the same way as the Tax Office or any other regulator; therefore their problem with the Regulator is not a Wolf as they initially thought.

I'm sure for some of you, this could be the start of a few A-ha moments.

There are six Wolves that commonly influence small businesses:

1. The word 'yes'
2. Cash flow
3. Staff (including contractors)
4. Technology
5. Time
6. Negativity

The word 'yes'

Think about how many times you say this word in a day – to yourself, your clients, your suppliers, and your family and friends. 'Yes, I can do that work in two weeks,' you may say, when you know you can't because you don't have the capacity or capability. Your reflex response is to say yes because you don't want to say no to the work, which means you might make a commitment to a client knowing you can't deliver the outcome.

Oh yes I can, I hear you say. But what if the cost is that in order to meet the commitment, you have to burn the candle at both ends and pay a heavy financial or personal price; be it reputation, health, family, time away from family and friends or possibly even making a loss on the job?

You might make a commitment to a member of staff by saying, 'Yes, you can go on holiday this week, no worries at all.' And then you look at the diary and think, hang on, a key project is due this week or, that's our busiest time.

I strongly encourage you to recognise this behaviour and start to change it. How, you ask? By stopping, taking a breath and considering what the consequences will be for you and your business before making any decision or commitment. Understand what the actual consequences will be if you say 'yes'.

Cash flow

This leads me to the second Wolf because saying yes, both positively and negatively, can influence cash flow. Cash flow is certainly another Wolf, often because it represents the big unknown.

In many businesses, particularly service-based businesses, cash flow can be quite inconsistent. Think about your own business. Does work slow down in December and January or is this your busiest time? Perhaps your clients are in their quiet period and need your assistance to get ready for the coming year? In retail for example, September and October are cash drains because businesses are purchasing their stock in readiness for the rush of Christmas shoppers.

Christmas/New Year is also a time when staff want to go on holiday and spend time with their families so how do you balance your cash flow when there is probably more money going out than coming in?

Do you know how much cash you need each month, each week? Or do you guess/pray/hope for the best?

Remember: Cash flow is the lifeblood of your business, just like electricity is essential to run your house.

Staff (including contractors)

This Wolf includes outsourcing tasks to 'virtual' options when the person is not physically located at your workplace and can include virtual assistants, graphic designers, bookkeepers and social media specialists. In these cases, there is often so much that's not written down in staff/contractor agreements such as performance reviews (when and by whom) and details of who pays for professional development; the smallest details can often undo your business.

What are the terms and conditions you are bound to once you have engaged someone to assist your business? How will they benefit your business? How will they provide the assistance? Do you have a get-out-of-jail-free option if you decide they're not the right fit for your business? Perhaps you don't really get on or there's doubt about whether they're delivering on the agreed outcomes within the timeframes or at the required standards.

If you use an external contractor or outsourcing option like a virtual assistant, have you formalised the agreement to ensure both parties are clear on expectations and boundaries? The written agreement should clearly outline what the person/organisation is going to do and what they are not going to do; what you will do and not do; how much they will be paid and when (e.g. all upfront, in progressive payments, monthly retainer); and when they have to complete and submit the work and documentation.

Contracts are insurance policies for your business. You only need them when something goes wrong, and in that moment, they become your bible.

These staffing issues may not be applicable to your business right now, but this will almost certainly become a critical component of your growth and ultimate success, and should be planned for well in advance as you continue to move to a Brick and/or The Reno business.

As mentioned above, it is crucial to get any agreements in writing. Handshake deals are often more about friendship than how long you have known the person or how much trust you have in the relationship. It's essential to have a written agreement, even if it's a simple one pager. As you will see in later chapters, the devil is in the detail. I would hate for anyone to make the same mistake I did years ago, and become unstuck or lose intellectual property. Instead of separating business and personal relationships, I based certain decisions on goodwill, thinking my friends would never do wrong by me.

Ensure your decisions are based on the information at hand at the time, and remember that sometimes a decision (even if it later turns out to be the wrong decision) can be better than no decision at all.

Sometimes you might find yourself thinking that if you just avoid the issue (the Wolf), it will go away. This doesn't always happen particularly if you have staff. I've found the majority of staff issues that business owners have are often unexpected or seemingly unimportant. Surprisingly, problems can arise around who does the washing up or cleans the kitchen. How tidy is your staff kitchen? Who has to clean the bathrooms and make sure they're tidy?

Staff kitchens and bathrooms can tell me so much about a workplace culture and leadership, often more than any conversation with business owners or members of staff. This can often be where frustration lies, which can hit the owner in the face or hide below the surface. But unless these Wolves are addressed promptly, team harmony and subsequent productivity can quickly unravel.

Technology

We live in an age and environment where we are expected to be available 24/7 and 'on' all the time. But it is your choice as to how you manage this particular Wolf. There is no need for anyone to entertain or accept this current environment of instantaneous response where we are expected to reply to an email within seconds of receiving it. I believe this is the warning sign to heed.

I suggest you move away from this unrealistic expectation. For one thing, don't you want to operate in a proactive manner rather than continually playing everyone else's game and thus running your business reactively?

Technology and emails are fantastic. I have my iPhone, iPad and now also a Surface tablet on which I wrote this book. I can always see what's coming into my inbox and whether I need to action anything. But I still have to have balance: balance in my business and how I allocate my time as well as balance in my personal life. I make sure I'm not available to my clients 24/7. I certainly respond to people in a timely manner, usually within twenty-four hours, and I provide as much value as I can for my clients at an exceptionally high level.

So who is really running your business? If it's your team and clients rather than you, think about how you can flip this. Where the Technology Wolf is concerned, think about what gadgets you have, how often you're on them, and how you use them. Can you turn off apps/software notifications so you only access these when you need to or really have the time?

If you can't live without your smartphone/tablet or without checking your emails for even five minutes, then I would seriously consider having a little intervention with yourself.

Time

Everyone has the same amount of hours in the day, but it's how those hours are prioritised which makes the difference between a profitable and productive business, and one that's always in survival mode.

I know you know you're not really time poor. Think about it. If you ask someone these days how they are, the response is usually, 'Oh, I'm *sooooo* busy.' And isn't this the reflex response you utter yourself when asked the same question? Of course it is and it could be true – to a point; your response is probably based on activity rather than what you should be doing to improve your business. Oh, and that very important activity of ensuring your business earns enough money to pay the bills (and yourself).

Negativity

Last, but certainly not least, is the Negativity Wolf which creeps into your thoughts, your words and your ultimate actions. You always have to be on the lookout for this Wolf which can appear from nowhere. Maybe it broke into your house in the middle of the night and stayed hidden in the shadows; or maybe it appeared in the people you associate with or listen to. Is this a Wolf you need to keep in check?

> Always be on the lookout for Wolves wanting to blow your business down

Reality Check

Every business owner, if they were honest, would admit they have at least one Wolf in their business they should keep at bay, even if they have a profitable business. And they probably also have at least one Wolf within themselves. My Wolf is procrastination which may surprise many who know me and have worked with me. I fight this Wolf sometimes once a week, sometimes once a day and sometimes even every hour, depending on what's happening in the business. For instance, I might get a bit bored with the first or last few steps of a task, or fight to get things started or completed.

Previously I had many tasks and projects, both in the business and at home, sitting at eighty-percent completion for a very long time. I probably started them feeling energetic, but by the end was over it and needed to move onto other things. Unfortunately though, the list just kept getting longer and I felt like I wasn't achieving anything. I was tired of the negative energy associated with having too many things still on the list so I began spending time at night and on the weekends completing the outstanding tasks that had been hanging around forever.

Every time I finished one of these tasks, I felt re-energised because I was finally able to take the Post-it note off the wall. And now, as I continue to chip away at them, I'm seeing fewer and fewer Post-it notes on the wall which means the finish line is in sight.

I've provided you with some real examples of Wolves in businesses, and maybe some of them also ring true for you (and you've put away your phone to concentrate on just reading my book). Or maybe there's another type of Wolf trying to blow your business down.

Many clients and workshop participants have told me their Wolves (aka threats to their business) are:

- The clock: not having enough hours in the day

- High expectations: of themselves, their clients and their staff

- An excess of paperwork necessary to maintain compliance particularly for those who work in a regulatory environment such as a registered training organisation

- Serving two masters at once: this can happen when reporting lines and relationships are not clear

- Doing too many things at once, with too broad a focus

- Being an expert in too many things at once rather than a generalist managing or leading other functions

- Procrastination or leaving things until the last minute

- Not being agile or adaptable to a rapidly changing environment and context

- Poor leadership skills with poor organisational communication between staff and external clients

- Organisational cultural issues

- The person who created the complicated system in the first place, be it paper or Excel

I particularly relate to the last one as I have a strong business systems background. One of my many talents (at times it's a curse) is being the checklist and flowchart queen. I've developed kits which document how people undertake just about any task in a business and this experience has demonstrated to me, time and time again, that people overcomplicate their processes. They put too much text into policies and procedures, past the point where they might be compliant or deemed necessary. A one page flowchart with a checklist of how to set up an event or place an order can achieve substantially more than twenty-seven pages in a procedure manual which will sit on a shelf collecting dust, or be buried deep in the electronic files, never to be looked at again.

Obviously it depends on your business, the industry sector and the size and nature of your enterprise, but the Wolves I've outlined are common in many businesses. Every owner and their teams should be mindful of them especially since they will creep up unexpectedly if business operations are not as well planned as they could be.

Now that I've outlined the many Wolves I see business owners fighting on a daily basis, can you identify the main Wolf you need to protect yourself and your business against right now? What materials do you need, strategies to employ to build a better business to stop the wind and the Wolf coming in the door?

Building your business ..... one brick at a time

1. What are your top three Wolves?

2. What is one thing you need to change about each Wolf to keep it at bay?

3. When will you start to make this change?

	My Wolf is ...	What is 1 thing I need to change to keep these Wolves at bay?	I will start making this change ...
Example	Procrastination	Develop Weekly Rituals including morning and evening tasks I will do every day	Tomorrow
Wolf 1			
Wolf 2			
Wolf 3			

Although time is a good indicator of the stage of development of any business, I have seen many that have been operating for as many as ten years and are still Straw businesses.

Material	Time in business
Straw	Start-up to 2 years
Stick	2–5 years
Brick	5–7 years
The Reno	Depends on how quickly Brick is achieved and/or the market changes
The Rundown	Anytime because the business owner either lost interest, had no idea or believed all was okay

What material do you think your business is currently built from?

☐ Straw

☐ Stick

☐ Brick

☐ The Reno

☐ The Rundown

☐ Not sure

☐ Don't want to admit to one yet

At least fifty percent of my clients and audience members start out thinking they are at the Stick stage, and it's only after further investigation they find out if this is true or not. It can be a shock to some business owners to discover how vulnerable their business really is, especially when it's clear they are still operating a Straw business. Some have been in business for several years but everything still revolves solely around them – something that can happen even when there are additional staff.

At this point in the book, you have determined if you are the Reluctant Business Owner and you have identified the Wolves you need to watch out for. In the next chapter, we move on from 'The Three Little Pigs' fairytale to my story of 'The Five Little Business Pigs' where you will discover there are two long lost brothers and that materials used to build houses often symbolise the various stages of a business.

Chapter 3

The First Little Business Pig
Straw

You read a book from beginning to end.
You run a business the opposite way.

You start with the end and then you do
everything you must to reach it.

Harold S Geneen

Now you have undertaken some soul searching to see if you really are the Reluctant Business Owner, and what your Wolf or Wolves may be, it's time to start looking at each of the business houses so you can determine what material your business is built of and the strategies you can start implementing to build stronger foundations; and thus have a thriving and enjoyable business.

If you have avoided the question of whether or not you are the Reluctant Business Owner, I strongly recommend you re-read Chapter 1 and answer the question honestly. Otherwise, there is no point in reading further because it is the basis of the concepts, steps and simple strategies I have outlined in this book to help you build a simple profitable business.

In the chapters covering the Five Little Business Pigs, I will describe each one as it pertains to the Business, People and Systems (BPS) model. This is to help you start building your BPS Roadmap for a simple, profitable business you love.

Please note the word 'people' is applicable whether or not you have staff. When I refer to 'people' throughout this book, I am referring to you as the business owner because you are the key person in your business; it also includes the people who help build your business either through ideas, support or completion of tasks. These people are those members of your team, be it onsite/virtual employees or contractors; as well as the people who provide support on an ad-hoc or as-needs basis, e.g. business consultant, accountability group, buddy or mentor.

Let's look at the characteristics of a Straw business to see if you are the First Little Business Pig.

Straw Business

Business	People	Systems
No Annual Business Plan (or it has been shelved)	Wearing every hat	Knowledge of business is in your head
Money is tight - business probably running at a loss and I don't really know my financials	Saying yes to everything and everyone	Very few procedures documented - probably only invoice and quote
Work coming from wherever and whomever - a scattergun approach	Available 24/7	No templates - copy and paste from one email to another

These **Straw Business** characteristics can be summarised by three key indicators:

1. It's all about one
2. Your day is primarily spent jumping from one task to another
3. Lack of planning

It's all about one

The first key indicator relates to a number of things. It's about one person doing everything in the business, whether that's you as the owner or one member of your team looking after a particular product, service or task. For example, it could be one building designer looking after commercial work or one trainer delivering all business training. This indicator means succession planning and back-up plans are a foreign concept which immediately puts your business at risk.

Too often, there is only one source of income for a business; be it government contracts, a long-term client or one product or service offering.

In the beginning, when a business is first set up, there will not be a lot of dollars floating around because the market of potential clients and partnership alliances don't yet know the business exists or what it does.

A Straw business can sometimes be identified as a start-up, either because the business has just commenced or because the owner has determined, like me, that this is their business model of choice. I do outsource a few activities such as IT support, but primarily all tasks and functions are performed by me: the business is *me*, clients engage *me*. This means that like many sole operators, I wear the 27,000 hats in my business.

Jumping from task to task

In a Straw business, the owner is also spending a lot of time jumping from task to task, often putting out fires because they're just reacting to whatever is happening in the business on that day. This usually means responding to whatever the client wants, reasonable or otherwise, because failure to do so could mean losing the work or client.

If there is a problem, you address it as best as you can but if you really looked at your behaviour, you're probably fixing 'to please' or make the problem go away (at least for today).

As a result, the business owner and the team are overworked. They are all putting in very long hours, as is common with any new venture, but there can be a kind of craziness going on where there is a lot of activity but not a lot of meaningful or tangible results. And because of the jumping from task to task and one idea to another, and the constant changing from 'I'll do this' to 'No, I'll do this instead', confusion instead of clarity runs rampant.

You may be lucky enough to have help in your Straw business. Your team may be happy to undertake long hours for a little bit because they believe in you, your passion and the difference you want to make. Remember, however, goodwill and passion without strong leadership and clarity will eventually run dry, and you will start to experience significant cultural issues.

Are the activities your staff are undertaking actually making a difference and achieving organisational goals and required outcomes or are they spending every day completing tasks that aren't really getting your business to where it needs to be?

Lack of planning

A Straw business that has no direction will often be short-lived, blown over easily through a number of factors:

- Lack of planning
- Bad decision making
- Poor leadership and management
- Change in the market
- High staff turnover and poor organisational culture
- Key person risk – the loss of a dominant client or staff member
- Poor outcomes and service delivery to clients, resulting in a damaged brand.

Did you know that 51 percent of all Australian small businesses close down within the first four years of operation?

Primary reasons for business failure include:

> Change begins with the first step

- Poor management
- Poorly designed business models or no business plan
- Lack of cash flow/capital
- Poor marketing
- Lack of financial knowledge

Source: Australian Bureau of Statistics and SmartCompany

Are these signs sounding familiar? Are they hitting too close to home? Maybe and maybe not. If you recognise your immediate issue, it may prompt you to wonder what you need to address immediately.

You may be feeling relieved that it's not you because you've been in business for ten years and you're still there. But length of time in operation is not necessarily the key indicator of a successful, simple, profitable business.

WHAT DO YOU WANT THEM TO DO?

One of my consulting clients wanted to take on a Virtual Assistant (VA) to answer the phone enquiries and undertake some administration duties which is a great idea when the dollars are available (or are just about to increase rapidly).

My first question was, 'What exactly will you get them to do?' The reply was, 'Hmm, I'm not sure.' My next question was, 'What information will you give them so they can answer the many questions potential clients will ask, keeping in mind you don't want these questions to keep coming back to you?' The answer was, 'I don't have anything like that.'

Solution

I then worked with my client to enable her to access all the information and procedures she kept in her head and wanted the VA to do. We slowly built up the VA kit for her business. This included a phone script on how to answer enquiries, a flowchart of sales enquiries, a template email to use with potential and existing clients and a template for daily tasks so she could communicate and track tasks quickly and easily.

The most valuable system in the kit was a comprehensive list of Frequently Asked Questions (FAQs). This was compiled by asking my client to brainstorm all the questions she was most commonly asked, either on the phone or via email. I then asked her each question and jotted down the answers. She tweaked them and after a few hours, the FAQs were done.

By developing this simple system, we achieved two key outcomes. Firstly, it meant the VA could answer the majority of potential clients' questions which in turn ensured my client could spend her time on more valuable, high revenue generating activities. Secondly, if the VA passed on an enquiry to my client, it was a warm sales call rather than a 'tyre-kicker' call. Over time, the VA continued to add any new questions and answers to the FAQ pages which assisted with future succession planning and outsourcing of tasks.

Building your business ..... one brick at a time

1. What are your top three Straw Wolves?

2. What is one thing you need to change about each Wolf to keep it at bay?

3. When will you start to make this change?

	My Straw Wolf is ...	What is 1 thing I need to change to keep these Wolves at bay?	I will start making this change ...
Example	Focus	Develop 1 Page Annual Business Plan	Tomorrow
Straw Wolf 1			
Straw Wolf 2			
Straw Wolf 3			

Do the indicators of a Straw business relate to you? If the Wolf hasn't blown your house down and your business is still standing, congratulations. Now we'll move onto the Second Little Business Pig to see if you have Stick foundations.

Chapter 4

The Second Little Business Pig

Stick

Your reputation is more important than your paycheck,
and your integrity is worth more than your career.
Angelo Sotira

ongratulations, you've survived your Straw business. Let's see if you're the Second Little Business Pig by examining some of the signs of the Stick business.

Stick Business

Business	People	Systems
Turnover may be okay but no idea of numbers so probably making a loss	Working 24/7 to cope with workload (even with help from employees or outsourcing)	Started documenting procedures but no structure or strategy so it's a fairly hit-and-miss approach
There is a plan but it's not very focused or achievable	Confusion about who does what = duplication	Many meetings held – very little achieved
Starting to build a regular client base but services and clients not clearly defined – helping anyone and everyone	Performance issues with staff – limited systems means that performance is hit and miss Majority of time spent answering phone calls, troubleshooting and fixing mistakes – in reactive mode versus proactive mode	Website up and running but not updated on a regular basis – latest news at least three months ago

These **Stick Business** signs can be summarised by three key indicators:

1. Bits of planning
2. Few solutions found
3. The band-aid effect

Bits of planning

There is *some* documented planning in place – more than in a Straw business where it's either non-existent or still in the owner's head. Hopefully, this planning has occurred because the owner has examined the reasons for the business' success rather than simply staying with the thought 'there is money in the bank so everything is all right'. This assumption is not always the case, and this line of thinking isn't sustainable, as shown in the following chapters.

Band-aided Solutions

The second and third indicators of a Stick business are linked because although these owners may look like they're solving problems; what they're actually doing is band-aiding issues, either in their business or for their clients. It's critical to ensure business owners look at the cause of each problem rather than just react to it.

There is more structure and substance within a Stick business than within a Straw business, but Stick businesses often find themselves unable to compete when a new competitor enters the

> Rip off all your band-aids to determine what's really costing your business time and money

marketplace or new technology changes the needs of their marketplace. Business owners operating a Stick business will have some grasp of financials and processes, but because they don't have their finger on the pulse of the marketplace, doors can be closed quite quickly, with the owner left flabbergasted, wondering what happened.

The operator of a Stick business will have developed *some* policies and procedures but may not have maintained or updated them since they were initially developed. This means they don't reflect the way the business operates if that business has moved on (at least in the owner's head if not on paper).

More dollars may be coming into the bank account but a Stick business is definitely not a sustainable, productive or profitable business. The result is the business has to be either shut down because it's not financially viable or left running like a mouse on the treadmill – stirring up energy but not really getting anywhere, hoping and praying for survival.

FLEXIBILITY CAN BE A CURSE

One of my clients had seven staff and although turnover was pretty good, she was quite frustrated and exasperated with her team. They were great people but some of them were not getting through their tasks as quickly as she would have liked; in fact, they were taking advantage of the flexibility she was providing in the workplace. Someone would email at eight am to say they were working from home that day instead of coming into the office, or someone else wasn't at work by their start time, and assumed it was okay to stay back later and make up the time.

I could certainly understand her frustrations. Unfortunately, I see this kind of situation often and it's due mainly to the close-knit environments created within small businesses. Everyone feels like they're all part of a family, and everyone including the owner is everyone else's friend rather than it being a place of business.

I believe it's very important and crucial to business success for people to get well and work as a team. But in this day and age of entitlement, I see more and more cases of staff stretching the boundaries with their employers and expecting more and more, often without giving anything extra themselves because they believe that's how a workplace should be.

Business owners need to think about how much they provide for 'free'; be it tea and coffee, new computers, printers and software, uniforms, celebratory lunches and outings … I could go on. But as many owners don't have the experience, skills or confidence to manage their teams effectively (and don't want to have the hard conversations as soon as issues arise), they often ignore or dismiss this behaviour. This can result in other team members feeling devalued because someone else is getting away with things.

Part of the reason this particular client's staff were taking liberties was because there were no position descriptions in place outlining the relevant tasks nor was there an organisational handbook to outline the dos and don'ts of working in this business including the relevant human resources/industrial relations information.

Solution

To address my client's frustrations and help her build a more sustainable and balanced business, I encouraged her to share with her staff all the information everyone needed to know. Previously, she had told her staff verbally how things were done but there was nothing written down. Together, we produced an organisation handbook containing the relevant Human Resources (HR) information about recruitment, induction, performance management, training, termination and resignation.

This Organisation Handbook was given to each staff member at a team meeting where the owner and I outlined key issues, re-established boundaries and announced expectations moving forward. As a result of this information being documented, staff now had a clear understanding of how the business operated and their roles within it. This handbook became the key tool for induction when new team members came on board, and it was also part of the performance management process.

By producing the handbook and explaining it to her staff at a team meeting, the owner made it clear she was taking control of her business. She did not single out those who hadn't been toeing the line, but I observed the dropping of certain heads at different times and it was clear the offenders knew who they were. By providing everyone with a clean slate, the owner was able to manage the performance of each individual from that point on, rather than remaining in an ongoing blame cycle which never achieves anything.

Q Building your business .....
one brick at a time

1. What are your top three Stick Wolves?

2. What is one thing you need change about each Wolf to keep it at bay?

3. When will you start to make this change?

	My Stick Wolf is …	What is 1 thing I need to change to keep these Wolves at bay?	I will start making this change …
Example	Financial viability	Review products and services to ensure each one is profitable	Tomorrow
Stick Wolf 1			
Stick Wolf 2			
Stick Wolf 3			

Do the indicators of a Stick business relate to you? If the Wolf hasn't blown your house down and your business is still standing, congratulations.

Now we'll move onto the Third Little Business Pig to see if you have built a Brick business.

Chapter 5

The Third Little Business Pig

Brick

Success seems to be connected with action.
Successful people keep moving.
They make mistakes but don't quit.

Conrad Hilton

Congratulations, you've survived your Stick business. Now let's see if you're the Third Little Business Pig by examining some of the signs of a Brick business.

Brick Business

Business	People	Systems
Know your numbers – great turnover, profit and cash flow	Clearly defined, documented roles and responsibilities because by now you will be more than a team of one	Procedures documented for every position within the business (even if you're doing every role)
Clear, achievable, documented annual business plan	Everyone loves coming to work, is engaged in their work and is doing their job well (including you)	Clients understand agreements and quickly complete simple but risk mitigating documents
Clear marketing messages and overall business clarity on what you do and how you do it	Formal and informal performance reviews occur with managed expectations and a high performing team	Minimal yet productive meetings and systems don't get in the way of performance – they enhance performance

These **Brick Business** signs can be summarised by three key indicators:

1. Strong leadership
2. Standard hours of work
3. Succession planning and a high performance team

Strong leadership

Within a Brick business, you as the owner demonstrate strong leadership across all facets of the business. Everyone in your team knows their job; everyone knows what they need to do to achieve success because you have outlined a simple and clear vision about what your business provides for its clearly defined client market.

Standard hours of work

Everyone in your team (including you) is working to the standard hours of work you have established for the business; be it nine to five, eight to four, 8.30am to 4.30pm or some other arrangement.

No one has to work late at night or on weekends to complete any required tasks. There may be a need to work an *occasional* extra hour here or there but the norm is everyone walks out the door at knock-off time feeling great because they achieved a lot that day.

'Not possible,' I hear you exclaim. 'How does this happen?' I hear you ask.

It's simple: documented systems and procedures are in place outlining who does what, to what required standard and by when. In addition, there are realistic and achievable timeframes which match a person's capacity and capability, and takes into account current workload.

I have mentioned this previously but I will continue to repeat it because it's the overarching theme of my book and also the concepts I instil in my clients and myself: after payment from clients for your product and services, *systems are the most important foundation to build into your business.*

Granted, systems do take a long time to develop but the investment of your time will definitely pay dividends in the long run. One of the best signs of a Brick business is that good systems are in place which means everyone is productive and work is completed within the standard hours of the workday.

Succession planning

And this is the bit I really like – there is succession planning in a Brick business. Anyone, including you as the owner, can step into another person's role and complete the required tasks, maybe not in the same way as the person who normally undertakes the role but at least accurately because everything the stand-in person needs to know has been clearly documented and is easy to follow.

This means there are backup technical staff who can step in to assist when a job needs it; backup administrative staff means more than one person can pay the wages; more than one accounts person; more than one person who can ... (insert the relevant role for your business). If someone calls in sick, there's a backup plan instead of the usual response of panic, cancelled meetings/training courses and so on which could lead to disruption in your business, frustrated clients and loss of income. I could go on with more examples but I'm sure you get the idea. Succession planning and well documented systems also mean staff are happy to help out and learn new things rather than feeling like they're being taken advantage of and devalued.

A Brick house also has very loyal clients. It has multiple income streams so not all its eggs are in one basket. Brick business owners have set indicators to track progress, and these determine whether the business is working or not and whether it's where it should be at any point in time.

A Brick business owner can also identify their position within the marketplace and stand toe to toe with their competitors (although they are not worried about competitors because they come from an abundance thinking pattern which means there is enough work for everyone). They are generating a decent amount of leads and are converting most of these, using ethical business practices.

> Plan your holiday breaks well in advance rather than taking a day here or there 'when I can'

The true test of a Brick business is when everyone, including you, has regular holidays without needing to check in mid-break. The business continues to provide consistent quality service to its clients and after a relaxing and rejuvenating holiday, no one returns to a nightmare of problems and piles of work.

GREAT TURNOVER DOESN'T ALWAYS INDICATE A BRICK BUSINESS

I see many small businesses fall into the trap of focusing on their turnover while failing to ensure they are operating the business as simply and productively as possible. One of my clients was an example of this.

The business employed twelve staff, lovely people who were fulfilling their roles as well as they could. But they were completing tasks in whatever way they liked, according to how they *thought* they should be done because very little was written down. The owner had told or shown them what to do, but this had never been translated into simple procedures.

Excuses included: 'We're too busy to do that,' and 'I don't want anyone to know my job because they might be able to do it better than me.'

Unfortunately, some people view knowledge as power and instead of wanting to share their knowledge, they remain guarded and keep it close to their chest (or in their head) as a self-preservation tool. This is a very dangerous modus operandi for any business but particularly a small business because that knowledge can walk out the door tomorrow.

Solution

To help the owner spend their valuable time gaining more business, I worked with each staff member to capture the knowledge out of their heads and put it into simple flowcharts and templates, outlining how they did their job. I then worked with the owner who tweaked and improved these processes. This meant that not only did the business have documented procedures for how the business should operate, but inefficiencies were also identified and then streamlined or eliminated altogether.

As a result, the business now had a strong succession strategy and backup plans for when a team member was sick, on holiday or simply wanted variety. The documented procedures also acted as a valuable induction tool for new staff members.

Now that I have described the Three Little Business Pigs and the indicators for each type of business, can you identify which Little Business Pig you are? Are you operating a Brick business, a Stick business or are you halfway between Stick and Brick?

When I work with new clients, I often find the business is a combination of more than one type: a bit of Straw, a bit of Stick and perhaps a bit of Brick. If this sounds like you, it may be time for you to consolidate to build a solid Brick business.

Thinking back on the signs for Straw, Stick and Brick businesses, has your decision changed from Chapter 2 as to the type of business you have really built?

Building your business .....
one brick at a time

1. What are your top three Brick Wolves?

2. What is one thing you need change about each Wolf to keep it at bay?

3. When will you start to make this change?

	My Brick Wolf is ...	What is 1 thing I need to change to keep these Wolves at bay?	I will start making this change ...
Example	Performance	Review staff performance to ensure boundaries and expectations are clear	Tomorrow
Brick Wolf 1			
Brick Wolf 2			
Brick Wolf 3			

Do the indicators of a Brick business relate to you? If the Wolf hasn't blown your house down and your business is still standing, congratulations.

If you're still unsure about which Little Business Pig you are, maybe you're holding back your final decision until you hear about the two remaining Business Pigs.

Now we'll move onto the Fourth Little Business Pig: The Reno (short for The Renovator).

Chapter 6

The Fourth Little Business Pig

The Reno

Opportunity is missed by most people because it is dressed in overalls and looks like work.
Thomas Edison

Congratulations, you've moved your business from Straw to Stick to Brick. Now it's time to take the next step (or maybe you're already there). Let's find out if you're the Fourth Little Business Pig and are renovating your Brick business.

There are three main reasons to renovate your business:

1. Meet the changing needs of the market and its clients
2. Chase opportunities or further scale your business
3. Re-energise and refocus

The Reno Business

Business	People	Systems
Diary fully booked or even oversubscribed	Owner's role changes from CEO to Managing Director – is not embedded in the business	Procedures continue to be streamlined and simplified, leading to scalability
Clients and partnership opportunities come to you	Investment in Business Development and Operations Manager positions	Procedures for new services are documented before they are launched
Lifestyle business – operates with minimal owner involvement	Team brings ideas for growth, and the systems needed to support it	Technology geared to efficiency – supports growth and sustainability

These **Reno Business** signs can be summarised by three key indicators:

1. Flexibility and speed to meet market demands

2. Everything and everyone comes to you (a blessing and a curse)

3. Culture of continuous improvement

Remember: Bigger isn't always better. It's important to keep your eye on the prize and focus on what your business model is (or should be) to achieve your goals and dreams. I've been

> Bigger isn't always better

astonished to see the number of owners who rapidly grew their businesses and then had to downsize for financial survival, either because they jumped on opportunities too quickly or took on additional staff because they believed that was the sign of success.

Why have these businesses failed to thrive? Generally for three reasons:

1. When the owner does the numbers, they discover they're working to pay their staff and nothing else so there's no money or profitability.

2. The owner is tired of spending most of their time dealing with client complaints and fixing mistakes which happen because they don't document their business systems before the business has grown (i.e. the owner thinks they're in a Brick business when really it's made of Straw or Stick).

3. The owner has jumped on every idea they have heard rather than staying true to the business model which suits them.

Oh, and another reason is many business owners realise they don't like managing staff.

I want to pick up on the business model point because this is the one which resonates with me the most. If I had a dollar for every time someone has told me to replicate myself and hire little minions so I could live the high life and only present occasionally, I would be a very rich person. But if I stopped speaking at conferences or running client workshops, I might as well shut the doors because this is what lights me up.

I do take on board the point they are making (in a roundabout way) which is: there are a maximum amount of hours in the day, and if I work all of them using a time-based business model, there is a ceiling to the amount of income I can earn.

This is very true. And this is why it's *essential* you find a way of replicating what you do. It could mean initiating procedures so you can engage more help which would enable you to step away from the day-to-day business operations. Or it could mean increasing financial revenue, perhaps by selling online so more people can access your products on a larger scale.

It could also involve podcasts, webinars, training programs and so on. I would add a word of caution regarding this option, however, because it still needs to fit into your desired business model, your personality and what you love to do; as well as conform to your current capacity and capability to branch out into a new field.

For me, podcasting is currently one of those 'you should do that' ideas. Although it's a good idea, after careful consideration, I've decided it's not in my plan at this time. However, I will still be part of this new technology by being a guest on podcasts my target market listens to which raises my profile without having to spend time creating new content and learning how to put together a podcast.

WE NEED A PROCEDURE FOR THAT

One of my clients is in a massive growth phase which is fantastic. This financial success is primarily a result of her perseverance and hard work, coupled with a strong understanding of systems being the key to substantially growing her business.

She has spent the necessary and painstaking time and money to develop simple systems. She has also stayed true to solving her clients' problems. She continues to do this by regularly asking her clients how her business can improve its services to them and testing price points to ensure the market will continue to pay for her products and services.

But the best thing – and this is when I knew real change had been implemented – is her staff not only come to her with exciting opportunities to consider but they also bring her financially viable solutions *and* documented systems and procedures to support the new initiatives.

My client has spent time educating her staff about the value of simple systems including how to write them using an agreed format and explaining why they are important.

Result: Her team sees and understands the value of business systems as the key to the success of her business, and they all want to continue building strong foundations to be part of that success.

Solution

This is the type of environment your business should be seeking; an environment of continuous improvement, which happens by default, because everyone working in the business wants to be part of its success.

Building your business ..... one brick at a time

1. What are your top three Reno Wolves?

2. What is one thing you need to change about each Wolf to keep it at bay?

3. When will you start to make this change?

	My Reno Wolf is …	What is 1 thing I need to change to keep these Wolves at bay?	I will start making this change …
Example	Growth	Review procedures to ensure quality of work is consistent for all clients, from all staff	Tomorrow
The Reno Wolf 1			
The Reno Wolf 2			
The Reno Wolf 3			

I have one more Little Business Pig to reveal and I truly hope this is not you. Some business owners become this Little Pig without realising it so it's important to be aware of the signs to make sure the Wolf is not closer than you think.

Let's take a look at the Fifth Little Business Pig: The Rundown.

Chapter 7

The Fifth Little Business Pig

The Rundown

We are what we repeatedly do.

Excellence therefore, is not an act but a habit.

Aristotle

The Fifth Little Business Pig is called The Rundown. How do you know if you're operating a Rundown business? Before I discuss the specific signs, I'd like to share with you some ideas on how you might 'suddenly' find yourself in a rundown business.

Warning: This chapter may contain confronting content, possibly causing you to throw the book down in disgust and say, 'That's not me.' Alternatively, it may (hopefully, if this is where you are at) provide the lightbulb moment and the push you need. Unfortunately, or fortunately, the truth hurts.

For me, this business house reminds me of a relationship. Remember when you met the love of your life and started dating, and that initial excitement on first meeting them? It's all about firsts:

- First look
- First touch
- First holding of hands
- First kiss
- First phone call

In the beginning, it's all consuming. You can't wait to see them again or talk to them on the phone; you're excited to receive a surprise text or email. This is the only person you want to be with ... all the time. Everything else you have to do slips down the To-Do list, plans get changed, excuses made. If you're lucky, your friends understand your constant postponements.

After dating for a while, many people take the next step in the relationship by moving in together and possibly getting married. There is energy and excitement again, although of a different kind, as you unpack yours and mine boxes to set up your joint home and you start getting used to each other in a different way.

After a while, things inevitably change. Life and routine set in. Perhaps you realise one day the excitement you felt when the love of your life came home isn't there as much, especially if you're no longer greeting them at the door with a kiss. You wonder what happened, where the romance and spark went. Love is still there but it seems harder to find time for just the two of you.

Let's interrupt this lovely walk down memory lane by replacing the person's name with your business name. Is the story the same?

For many of my clients and my audience members, this is an unfortunate but familiar tale. As I've previously described, for many business owners, the journey begins with them putting all their time and energy into their business because it totally consumes them: it is *everything* to them. But somehow, somewhere along the way, they become complacent and lose some of that passion and focus.

That's when the hard work really begins because they have to dig in. Why? Because they start questioning themselves, with the accompanying feelings from the Negativity Wolf:

- Why did I start this business?
- Is this really why I left my job?
- Why is this happening?
- I'm working so hard so where's the cash?
- Etc. etc. etc

I certainly understand this situation as it's a place I've visited on more than one occasion since I commenced my business in 2002.

Do you want an expensive hobby or a profitable business?

Whether you like it or not, if you want to survive in business these days, you have to keep changing how you operate. If you don't embrace social media and changes in technology and the working environment, you risk turning into The Rundown Little Business Pig – if you're not there already. And if you're not careful, you risk turning into the Sixth Little Business Pig which is the Closed business (as per Borders and Kodak).

So let's see if you're the Fifth Little Business Pig by examining the signs of a Rundown business (when reading this chapter, it's important you really connect with what you're thinking and feeling):

The Rundown Business Owner (You):

- You're fed up and exhausted

- You're no longer in love with your business

- You believe everything is okay, even though the evidence tells a different story

The Rundown Business

Business	People	Systems
Dollars may show acceptable turnover but there's little or no profit – could even be close to bankruptcy	Disgruntled, bored, confused, frustrated, lost interest and energy – poor organisational culture	Clients don't come back as often or at all – no follow-up as to why
Energy isn't being directed into looking for new clients	High staff turnover	Business hasn't been updated/streamlined for at least a year
Blinkers on – opportunities are being missed	Focus is on doing the same work – no improvement or innovation	Mistakes keep happening – covered over rather than looking at the cause

The ultimate sign of The Rundown Business is everything is a mess – your office, your desk, your files and your headspace. Lack of clarity means you don't know which way to turn or what to do next to keep your head above water today, let alone survive the week.

You might think you're running a great business, but the signs of a Rundown Business can sneak up on you. It's only when you look at your Business, People and Systems, both in isolation and holistically, that you can see the real holes in the Brick (or the Straw or Stick).

Too often a business is run like a hobby or old-fashioned charity rather than a profitable enterprise. Any business including a not-for-profit has to make money to at least pay the bills and keep services operating. But in many situations, the owner gets so caught up in the idea of running a business solely around doing what they love that they ignore the numbers and keep ploughing money into it: in essence, flogging a dead horse (this is also one of the signs of the Reluctant Business Owner).

Anyone can have an awesome idea. But if you keep giving that idea away and can't find people who actually want to *pay* for that idea (as opposed to those who say thank you but don't show you any money), you're not actually running a business. Instead, you have an expensive hobby and I suggest to you it's time for a rethink. (By the way, there's nothing wrong with an expensive hobby if you can still pay your bills and have no financial issues.)

If any of this chapter is ringing true for you, isn't it time to draw a line in the sand and make the tough decision? Either close down the business or make the necessary changes to turn it around.

Building your business .....
one brick at a time

1. What is your decision: close or change?

2. What is one thing you need to do to either close down your business or change your method of operation?

3. When will you start to make this change?

Decision	One thing I need to change to make this decision a reality	I will start making this change
Close		
Change		

Now you've determined which Business Pig you are (and I hope you're one of the first four Little Business Pigs and not the fifth), it's time to see if you're also a M.A.D. Business Pig.

Chapter 8

Are you running a M.A.D. Business?

If you aren't making a difference in other people's lives,
you shouldn't be in business.

Sir Richard Branson

Now you've determined what kind of business you've built, it's time to consider one more material to include in your foundations.

This material is *SERVICE*.

I believe, without a doubt, that most people want to Make A Difference (M.A.D.) in all they do; whether it's with their family and friends, their business or their wider community, and I am no different. I'm very driven by *SERVICE* and helping people, so much so that it's in everything I do.

I credit my parents for their amazing example. They have always given their time to whomever needed it, whether it was a family member or friend; my schools (tuckshop, planting trees, working bees), or my netball teams (Dad as coach, Mum as manager and they were on the Committee). They have always helped out at our church and in the wider community which has continued into their retirement (including Dad erecting the Christmas lights for our huge festival and Mum singing, baking and working on the stalls).

If I listed everything my parents have undertaken in a volunteer or service capacity in their lives, or even just what they're still doing in their retirement, this book would have many more pages.

My point is by having such strong and fantastic role models, being of service to others and volunteering my time is something I don't think twice about because it's all I've known: in my family, it's just what we do.

It's this service culture which has drawn me to working with organisations aligning with this philosophy, so much so that the majority of my life as an employee has been with government and not-for-profit organisations with a strong community and volunteer focus. It's these values which draw me to potential clients in three sectors: government, private and not-for-profit. Sometimes, however, this ethos and drive can be my downfall and I can give away too much of my time and knowledge.

For me, being a M.A.D. person is a given, but unfortunately not everyone or every business owner has this philosophy at the forefront. And I wonder why that is? I think it's important to work out whether this is part of a person's DNA (like me) or whether they have just forgotten and need a gentle reminder. I know and understand how this can happen especially when people become busy or money is tight.

I've outlined in previous chapters how a business should be simple, profitable and, if possible, serve its clients, members of staff and the community. As the word *service* can often mean different things to different people, I will explain what I mean by this word and why it's an essential material to building a M.A.D. business.

Service means so much more than helping people and great client service. It's about ensuring everything serves a purpose and is done to Make A Difference rather than simply completing an activity or task for the sake of it.

Henry Ford said, 'A business that makes nothing but money is a poor business'. There are many questions that need to be asked before the M.A.D. concept can be used to benefit a business, its people and its systems.

Business

- Is money for material things your sole focus?

- Are relationships more important to you than money?

- Do you give back to your clients, your team and your community? If so, how often?

Examples of M.A.D. business practices include rewarding staff (as individuals or collectively) with movie vouchers, gold class screenings, cooking classes, barefoot bowls, a day at the races or putt-putt mini golf; all of which are great team building activities for a job well done. Businesses can also choose to support a charity or sponsor a sporting team for one year e.g. Australia's Biggest Morning Tea, Free Dress Friday, Jeans for Genes Day, pink ribbons for Breast Cancer, Movember, Bridge to Brisbane etc.

You may also want to look at something like B1G1 (Buy1Give1: Businesses for Good at www.b1g1.com where every business transaction (e.g. each time you make a sale), you can donate a proportion of that sale to an international charity or project of your choice. For example, I know of a library education RTO which donates money (in the form of bricks) to a community in Tanzania to build a community library every time a student starts another subject in their qualification. But there are hundreds of projects you can choose from donating water to a child in India, to a young orphan in Thailand getting access to education, or a family in Nepal getting a goat to create a sustainable income. The list is endless ...

It's important to bear in mind not everyone wants money as a reward. We experience our best rewards through activities like giving other people

> **Not everyone wants money as the reward**

experiences they couldn't otherwise afford, or contributing to something bigger than our jobs, our businesses or ourselves.

People

- Are you actively listening to and regularly seeking feedback from your team, and then taking on board any of their suggestions?

- Are you actively listening to and regularly seeking feedback from your clients, and then taking on board any of their suggestions?

- Does everyone in your team provide exceptional client service, every single time?

So many business owners tell me they want feedback: from their accountability group, their mentors, their team and their clients. But when they're told some truths they don't like rather than acknowledging the issues and using the knowledge to build better businesses, often they either ignore the ideas or dismiss them entirely.

If this sounds like you, my question to you is: Why are you asking for feedback or ideas if you have no intention of accepting that there may be some truth in what you hear or even a golden nugget?

Think of the three wise monkeys. The first has its eyes covered, the second has its ears covered and the third has its mouth covered. The statue can represent the concept of turning a blind eye or dismissing things or refusing to get involved.

For those business owners who operate like this, I ask you to participate in a fake consultation process. Imagine I have asked you for ideas. I make it appear I care about you and your ideas but I have no intention of listening to anything you say or doing anything with your ideas and information.

Can you see how a process like this could lead to staff and clients complaining, suffering in silence or simply leaving? None of these outcomes are great for business.

What's even worse is when a business promises a client the world. Excited, the client signs up, believing the business holds the answer they have been seeking. When those promises are not met, the new client becomes disenchanted, leaves and speaks negatively about the business to others instead of being a raving fan.

I'm sure you know word of mouth can either kill or boost a restaurant. It's the same with any business. I'm still seeing businesses ignoring their clients once they've signed on the dotted line and handed over the cash to focus on the next signature and the next.

Unfortunately, this is a common occurrence in the training or professional development arena, something I have experienced personally. Before I signed up with this particular company, they assured me they would help me with anything I needed to be successful. But once they had my money, my status and value changed completely. They went from saying they would help me to silence. Or they told me they would indeed help me, but first they needed more money. Instead of valuing me as a client who could provide a constant referral base, they chose to either ignore me or dismiss me outright and instead continued to focus their time and energy on gaining new clients. And once they had their money from those clients, the cycle started again.

Remember: It is financially five to seven times more expensive to gain a new client than to look after an existing client base who can also be a fantastic referral opportunity.

So where is your focus? Are you valuing your current clients or are you chasing the next big thing? Does your focus need to change? Treat your clients right, serve them well and you will be amazed at what comes back to you.

Systems

- Do your systems including policies and procedures serve their intended purpose and make sense to everyone who reads them, whether they are your clients or your team? For example, how easy is it for your staff to apply for leave?

- Do your systems make it easy for clients to do business with you? For example, how many pages are in your contract or client engagement forms? If they are more than three pages, is every word needed or does it include waffle?

- Do your systems annoy your clients or your staff?

I want to pick up on the last question because it's high on my frustration list. In this age of automation, I can appreciate how technology can assist businesses and their clients. But unfortunately I see too many examples where the exact opposite happens particularly in the event management space. I sign up to events and receive so many reminder emails and SMS messages which drives me nuts. Why can't I be treated like the responsible person I am? If I book an appointment or advise I'm attending an event, it goes straight into my diary. I note the time and place and I turn up. In addition, as there are a number of annoying nuances that have come with automation technology e.g. multiple emails/SMSs to book in for events I'm attending, reminders to RSVP days before the RSVP deadline and asking me to rate events I didn't attend. Please look at your systems to ensure you are not annoying your current and potential clients.

Don't blame the system

Stop blaming the 'system' for these issues. Either fix the back-end setup, train people to use the technology properly or performance manage those people who *choose* not to follow the system correctly.

Everything you do in your business including your procedures and how you treat others, should make a difference and be as simple as possible. If this is not happening, then review the system and improve it to ensure both staff and clients find it easy to work with you and for you.

I came across this quote a few years ago and I have it blown up on my office wall, just in case I ever lose my way. It not only sums me up to a T but is a fitting way to end the M.A.D. Chapter.

I slept and dreamed that life was happiness.

Then I awoke and found out that life was service.

I served and I found out that in service, happiness is found.

Rabindranath Tagore, Nobel Laureate 1913

Building your business ..... one brick at a time

1. Are you a M.A.D. Little Business Pig or do you have some Wolves you need to address?

2. What is one thing you need change about each Wolf to keep it at bay?

3. When will you start to make this change?

	My M.A.D Wolf is ...	What is 1 thing I need to change to keep these Wolves at bay?	I will start making this change ...
Example	*Generosity*	*Maintain a balance between profitability and helpfulness*	*Tomorrow*
M.A.D. Wolf 1			
M.A.D. Wolf 2			
M.A.D. Wolf 3			

It's now time to help you get CLEAR on your Business, People and Systems (BPS). Part Two is all about building your BPS Roadmap for the simple, profitable business you love.

Part Two

Build your BPS Roadmap

Take the first step in faith.
You don't have to see the whole staircase,
just take the first step.

Dr Martin Luther King Jnr

Chapter 9

Business
What the ...

You have to be ready for hard work and frugal spending
to get the idea off the ground.

Garrett Camp

kay, so you've reached this point and maybe there have been some A-ha moments along the way, maybe a few nods of agreement and even a tear or two, some deep breaths and sighs; and now you're ready to embark on a different journey.

Let me assure you that it's going to be okay. You've identified the material your business is made of and discovered which Business Pig you are at the moment which is great. Now it's time to identify any mistakes you may have made (and those to avoid) as part of building your BPS Roadmap for the simple, profitable business you love.

The next two chapters will look specifically at your People and your Systems. First though, it's important to look at where business owners often go wrong as they start building their business and then you can determine your next step.

How many of the following common business mistakes apply to you? It's important to self-reflect honestly on these mistakes to determine if they relate to you because unless you know where you are now, you can't determine the best step forward which will take you where you need to go. Be honest with yourself as you review the seven mistakes so you can be the best business owner possible.

Self-denial will only put you back on the treadmill which you really don't want.

> Self-denial only puts you back on the treadmill

MISTAKE #1: KNOWING THE WHY BUT NOT KNOWING (OR HAVING) THE HOW

Many business owners lack a clear understanding of what their business is about. They might know why they started the business (or think they do) and maybe they understand a little of how this will be achieved. However, there's no clarity, no knowledge of what they actually do, how they do it or what their specific target market is really.

Does this describe you and your business?

Sometimes businesses are established purely because funding was available, a common occurrence within the vocational education and training (VET) sector. 'Hey, let's just go and grab the cash and provide that training' becomes the sole reason the business exists.

When I moved from being second in charge to CEO of the Forest Industries Industry Training Advisory Body (FITAB), I asked a key question at my first board meeting: 'Can you please tell me why we're here?' The answer I received was 'because DET [the state government] funds us'. To which my response was: 'Can we please shut the doors now because that's *not* why the organisation exists.'

I was met with perplexed stares and wonder at my boldness (and I'm sure a few people wondered if they had appointed the right person). Funding, I assured them, was important but it was only one component and one function undertaken by the ITAB. The organisation was *actually* there to educate people in the industry about the importance of having highly trained people in their businesses; and help these businesses to gain training opportunities to upskill their workforce. The DET contract was a small financial but time intensive component of these activities.

Within the many businesses I've consulted for and the business owners with whom I network, there are many that cannot clearly and succinctly articulate what they do and why they do it. It can be hard because business owners are focused on the money rather than the market.

Result: They are often being everything to everyone because they haven't defined a clear niche market.

Within your industry sector, have you identified the specific markets or type of clients you work with? Could you clearly define to another businessperson at a function or even at the BBQ with friends the specific clients you work with and why? Or are you being everything to everyone? Continuing with this strategy will only take time and energy away from those key, most profitable clients who will help you build a profitable business because you will be selling a commoditised product or service, which won't get you very far.

If you have a lack of clarity about what you do, you probably don't have a real plan to achieve the ultimate vision and purpose of your business. Many businesses don't have a business plan written down, or if they do, it might be highly complicated. A 60 page document might be ideal for a bank loan to establish credibility and long-term projections but hopeless in real life as a practical document which helps you keep your eye on the prize. Or maybe you have one but it is woefully out-of-date because it hasn't been reviewed since you started your business, let alone in the last year.

Which do you identify with: no plan or one that's so complicated and/or out-of-date, it's been shelved?

If you're not able to put down on one page the key priorities for the business this year and identify how each priority will be achieved, I strongly suggest your Annual Business Plan needs a re-think (I have outlined a few simple solutions to solve this issue in Chapter 19).

Without a plan for achieving XYZ, trust me, you will get consumed by daily tasks and distractions and become so overwhelmed that you cannot see the wood for the trees. At this point, many business owners put their head in the sand. But head in the sand = blindness. You can't be successful without seeing what's happening right in front of you.

And now you need to determine if your business is really a business.

MISTAKE #2: CREATING A HOBBY RATHER THAN A BUSINESS

The second common business mistake is when the owner operates the business as a hobby instead of a profitable business. Why a hobby? Simple: hobbies don't usually make money. So if your business isn't making money, it's still in the hobby phase (and possibly an expensive one at that). And regardless of what people might tell you, you cannot live on passion or air alone.

Whether you're working in your own business, a not-for-profit organisation or for the government; there still has to be money coming in the door, consistently, to pay the bills. As I will address further in the book, too many business owners don't know their financial numbers as they work their passion.

If you're *not* running your business to make money, then you're not a business owner. You simply have a nice hobby, and for some people, that's all they want which is fine. But if you are a business owner, you want to make money: it's the primary reason you started a business in the first place.

How much money you want to earn is entirely up to you. Obviously you want enough to pay the bills and have your desired lifestyle. Otherwise what are you doing? I know I want to make money so I can help my family and undertake my M.A.D. activities.

If you don't want to run a business which makes money, please get out now. Sell the business and retire, get a job that makes you happy or employ someone who wants to make money *and* knows how to make money to operate the business.

How does someone fall into not looking at the finances? Often, it's because they get excited when clients work with them but unfortunately, they miss the Yes Wolf and fall into the trap of overpromising.

MISTAKE #3: OVERPROMISING AND UNDERDELIVERING

How many times have you promised a client's work will be completed by a specific date, only to have poor planning on your part as well as unexpected circumstances, mean the deadline wasn't met? Have you then contacted the client, explained the situation and accepted ownership of the situation? Or have you avoided the conversation and completed the work in your timeframe?

Think about it: what is your usual modus operandi in this situation? How many phone calls (excuses) do you make in a day? How many times has a staff member not told you about a mistake they made and instead covered it up, only for you to find it inadvertently? Overpromising and underdelivering follows the same mistake process.

Now put yourself in your client's shoes. How many times have you paid money for a product or service that hasn't been delivered as expected? How did you feel? Do you want your clients to have this same feeling and disappointment? Overpromising and underdelivering is often the path businesses take their clients down, and then they wonder why they don't have enough repeat business or ongoing referrals.

Unfortunately I see this mistake too often. Why? Experience shows me business owners don't want to admit they can't service their commitments, behaviour which is then modelled by their team. They fail to be accountable for their mistakes and don't accept the responsibility and subsequent consequences; blaming staff, the system or anything except themselves.

I understand mistakes happen because no one is perfect. However, as I tell my junior netball team when they throw the ball away or miss a goal, it's what you do next that's most important.

A colleague of mine says, 'You can't change the past but you can create the future.' How you proceed is up to *you*. Don't promise something you may or may not be able to deliver. Ask the person when they want it and how. If you then commit, understand you can't renegotiate down the track because you've accepted the terms and conditions.

Remember: When mistakes happen, own them quickly and honestly by genuinely explaining what happened and move on. Don't wallow in the mess because this will only make it worse.

MISTAKE #4: IT'S A MESS

I'm not suggesting your primary work area (desk, office, kitchen, construction site etc.) looks like a disaster area, but having an untidy work area is not only about your physical space; it's also about the space in your mind.

I'm not here to tell you that everyone has to have a neat and tidy work area at all times because mine certainly isn't every single day, especially if I've been away travelling. However, I know from research and experience that working in a cluttered space and with a cluttered mind often results in people spinning their wheels, jumping from task to task because they can't see what to do next.

Does this sound familiar? If this is you, this situation will be further exacerbated if there's no clarity in your business focus.

It also doesn't make a good first impression if clients see clutter on desks, floors and in other commonly used areas. This might seem a small issue to be concerned about as you run your business, but let me assure you, the devil is in the detail.

MISTAKE #5: THE DEVIL IS IN THE DETAIL

The devil is absolutely in the detail. You might not have recognised this message in the 'Three Little Pigs' fairytale but I'm sure it was aligned with the Wolf.

How many times have you checked a fee proposal before presenting it to a client and realised, after the fifth read, it was missing an entire section or a figure was missing an extra zero? Leaving off a zero could be a costly mistake if the proposal is sent to the client without picking up the mistake. Do you feel your stress rising because you've been here before?

Why does this happen? Many people believe giving their work to someone to check is a sign of weakness. But I can assure you, the weakness is in *not* having your work checked. When you develop your own material, you're too close to it which means you see what you want to see rather than the detail written on the page. I'm a qualified proof reader and I still miss errors in my own work. This is why I invested in professional services to edit this book: just like top sports players have coaches to keep an eye on their skills.

When I initially set up my business in 2002, my business card didn't have either my email address or mobile phone number. Everyone had looked at it including the graphic designer, and we all missed it (luckily it did have the website address). The oversight happened because we were all too close to it; we had looked at it too many times so we only saw what we *thought* was there, not what was *actually* there.

We see what we want to see, and we do this more often than we like to admit. What's your approach to checking your work?

> We see what we
> want to see

I suggest you realise the value of the detail and find someone other than the Wolf to assist you and your business.

MISTAKE #6: YES PLEASE

As I alluded to earlier, business people have a tendency to say yes to everything. *Yes, I can complete a tender for you by tomorrow, not a problem.* Except you've never done this before and already have six hours of work to be completed by the end of today.

Business people often agree to do something without first taking a breath and thinking about what it means for them: from logistics to finances to resources. Why? Because they think it's poor client service to say no. Sometimes it happens because they simply want to provide service to that client but if they're not clear about the details, it can cost far more than the total bill. It can cost ongoing business, starting with the client they really wanted and extending to all the potential clients they have lost when the disappointed client tells others about the poor service they received.

Business owners also say yes because they want to be everyone's friend and be the 'good' boss, but before long even their team members are saying yes too often because everyone in the business wants to be seen as nice. But what's the point of being nice in business if yes really means maybe and maybe leads to no?

Saying yes is a great overarching principle but there are times when a tough call is needed. Sometimes you need to have the hard conversation with yourself, your team, your clients and your family; and use the two-letter word *no*. Saying yes to everything might mean that eventually your Brick business empire will be visited by the Wolf and it will all come tumbling down; leaving your health, money and relationships in a pile of rubble.

Instead of saying yes all the time, you would be better off taking a breath to determine whether saying yes to what the person is asking is really the best decision for you and your business, both now and in the future. When you say NO; state it honestly, respectfully and calmly, in the same manner you would like to be treated. You'll be surprised. Not only will you feel good about your decision, but you'll also like the way it instils respect in your clients and your team.

MISTAKE #7: HARE VERSUS THE TORTOISE

The last of the big business mistakes follows on from mistake #6. We often act as the hare and not the tortoise because we believe that quicker is better in our fast-paced society. Wrong!

I keep reinforcing this concept with the netball teams I coach: be the tortoise and not the hare. My team is often not the fastest but I do my best to make it the smartest on court. This is important because the key to netball is reading the play and anticipating the next few moves so the team can intercept and score the winning goal.

I'm not saying you have to take forever to make decisions or complete tasks. What I am saying is that rushing to complete everything in five seconds is when mistakes occur. These actions cost businesses dearly, not only in their decision making and finances but also, importantly, in their reputations.

I don't know about you but I have days and weeks where clients and colleagues don't take the time to read my text messages or emails properly. This drives me nuts because my message is often misinterpreted or the reader just gets it totally wrong. Does this also happen to you? How do you feel?

I once sent a client an email letting them know I could meet them on one of three specific dates and times, and I offered choices to make it easier for them to know when I was available. The response the client sent back read: *That would be great. What* would be great? Which day would be great? What time would be great? (I told this story at a conference and the organiser mumbled a very loud 'Sorry!' This elicited a deserved laugh from the audience as well as confirmation from me that he wasn't one of the perpetrators.)

It takes five seconds to stop and read an email or text message to see what has been suggested or requested. Think about the lack of productivity and the lost opportunities occurring in your business from a series of backwards and forwards text messages and emails. Texts and emails not only cost time and money but sometimes businesses trade this inefficiency for the sake of their reputations. Why keep working with someone who has such disregard for your time? How long are you going to keep being the busy hare?

How often have you sent an email and then uttered 'oops'? There is a classic moment in the movie *The Intern* when Anne Hathaway's character is doing too many things at once on her phone and inadvertently sends an inappropriate email to her mother instead of her colleague. It's hilarious to see the lengths her team goes to in order to prevent her mother from seeing her email. It's funny in a movie but not so funny when it happens in your business.

DON'T PLAY THE GAME

I was asked at a conference I was presenting at if I had a way to stop the busyness of the hare and to 'politely tell people who don't read their emails and information that they are a knucklehead'.

I responded by saying some of it is actually about raising the conscious awareness of everyone, including ourselves, to highlight this behavioural pattern. Having a simple visual trigger like a stop sign on your desk and phone can go a long way towards moving you from reaction to conscious thoughtful behaviour.

You do have to tell people, politely, so they know what they're doing and why it's annoying and counterproductive. It's also about educating clients and teams about their actions and behaviours. I wrote the following the first time it happened: *As per my email below, can you please advise which date and time we will be meeting?*

My colleague takes a different approach. She'll respond by taking control of the situation, replying to the email with a meeting appointment, confirming she understands all the options are favourable, and selecting the meeting date and time which best suits her. This then gives the other person a way to refuse or change the meeting and avoid email ping-pong.

If, for some reason, the message still doesn't get through, I then pick up a phone and have a conversation. I need to make sure I'm not making the assumption that I've written it 'incorrectly'.

I also believe it's important to educate people about the ineffectiveness of email and text tag which we can quickly get into. It's also about understanding protocols: how often and how much you reply via email or text messages. For example, if someone thanks you in an email, you don't need to reply to that email to say thanks for the thank you email. Otherwise, you'll spend your day exchanging thank you messages.

Solution

Back to the original question I was asked. I would initially frame my response by outlining in the first email the information the recipient had missed to gain the desired response. If they still didn't read or respond appropriately, I would give them a call for two reasons (I do my best not to get into email or text tag):

1. To make sure it was their error and not mine. If it was me, I would fix the problem immediately.

2. To express my concern that they were not reading my emails properly, and ask if it was because of the way I had written or was there something else?

According to their responses, I could then determine the true cause of the problem.

It's important to work with your clients and your team to help them understand how you do business. This not only ensures they are the right fit for you and your business, but means they also understand your processes and communication methods and can feel confident you are the right fit for them.

Generally, short, succinct emails are best but I have to be careful because I can sometimes be a little too succinct. As a result, my emails can come across as quite blunt which is not the intent.

Some time ago, when I had been working on a project to provide feedback on training materials, in my usual efficient style, my reports were bullet points – *very* succinct. Following the submission of one of these reports, I had to have a conversation with some of the content writers to explain it wasn't their writing style I was critiquing; it was me saying *I work with businesses every day and this is what they're looking for as part of that process.*

Moral of the story: communicating via email and text may seem quick and efficient, but it's important to match your communication medium to your audience and educate them about how you work. Liaise with people: take care not to write or say too much (although too little can also be misinterpreted and waste time, the very time you want to save).

It's important to take on board this communication concept and look at the emails you've sent to your internal and external team. There's no need to begin with a salutation, instead just launch into your message: *Reviewed client report. Please follow up with client on Tuesday.* Many of us were taught that 'Dear Jake' is the polite way of beginning a letter, but times have changed and the etiquette is now different for technology based communications.

Help your staff to understand that emails should be written like this to increase productivity. Otherwise they may get offended at the lack of the usual email small talk and they may assume (incorrectly) that you're not happy with them which, in turn, could make them think they've done something wrong (again incorrectly).

Education is the key so ensure it happens because time is money. I encourage you to think of the number of times you have been the hare, rushing about and wasting time. What has this rushing to the finish line really cost you?

Building your business ..... one brick at a time

1. What are your top three Business Wolves?

2. What is one thing you need change about each Wolf to keep it at bay?

3. When will you start to make this change?

	My Business Wolf is ...	What is 1 thing I need to change to keep these Wolves at bay?	I will start making this change ...
Example	*Clutter*	*Declutter office and desk*	*Tomorrow*
Business Wolf 1			
Business Wolf 2			
Business Wolf 3			

Now you know the Business mistakes in your BPS Roadmap, let's look at the People mistakes to determine what's really costing your business time and money.

Chapter 10

People
Help or Hinder?

People do not decide to become extraordinary people.
They decide to accomplish extraordinary things.

Sir Edmund Hillary

Ask business owners about managing people or 'having staff' and most roll their eyes and start on a huge rant about their staff not doing what they are asked. The response usually includes comments like 'I thought my staff would help me but I spend all day dealing with their problems so they're just costing me money'; hence the title of this chapter.

In order to build your roadmap for a simple profitable business, it's critical to examine the people aspect to see if it's in balance with your

Business and your Systems. The word *people* is a useful collective noun to encompass several key areas:

- Staff or team – whichever is your preference
- You – if you are a team of one
- Contractors, suppliers, outsourced options, consultants
- Anyone else who helps your business (full time, part time, paid, unpaid etc.)

I am constantly amazed by the number of clients who engage me to deal with someone who is causing them 'problems'. Yet W Edwards Deming tells us ninety-four percent of all failure is a result of the system, not the people. Why does the rhetoric not match the facts?

Most business owners believe their main problem is their staff, but it's not. Initially, it can either be an issue within the business or a lack of simple systems because the knowledge remains in people's heads or procedures are so complicated no one follows them anyway; or both.

Work Personality Types

You may be familiar with the many personality profiling tools available to help CEOs, Managers and Recruiters determine the best person for a position, based on their skills and personality, and how they will fit with existing team members and the culture of the business. These tools include DISC, Myers Briggs and the Hermann Brain Dominance Instrument (HBDI) which I highly recommend.

However, you may not be as familiar with the Oz Model of Work Personalities, developed by Dr John Evans and Christina Afors, as part of the Australian Quality Council – Cultural Imprint Study in 1994 which was funded by Telecom (now Telstra).

This model identifies both the level of happiness and the willingness to express this in the workplace, and outlines progression (or regression) between four different work personality types: Prisoner, Survivor, Whinger and Volunteer.

Which work personality are you?

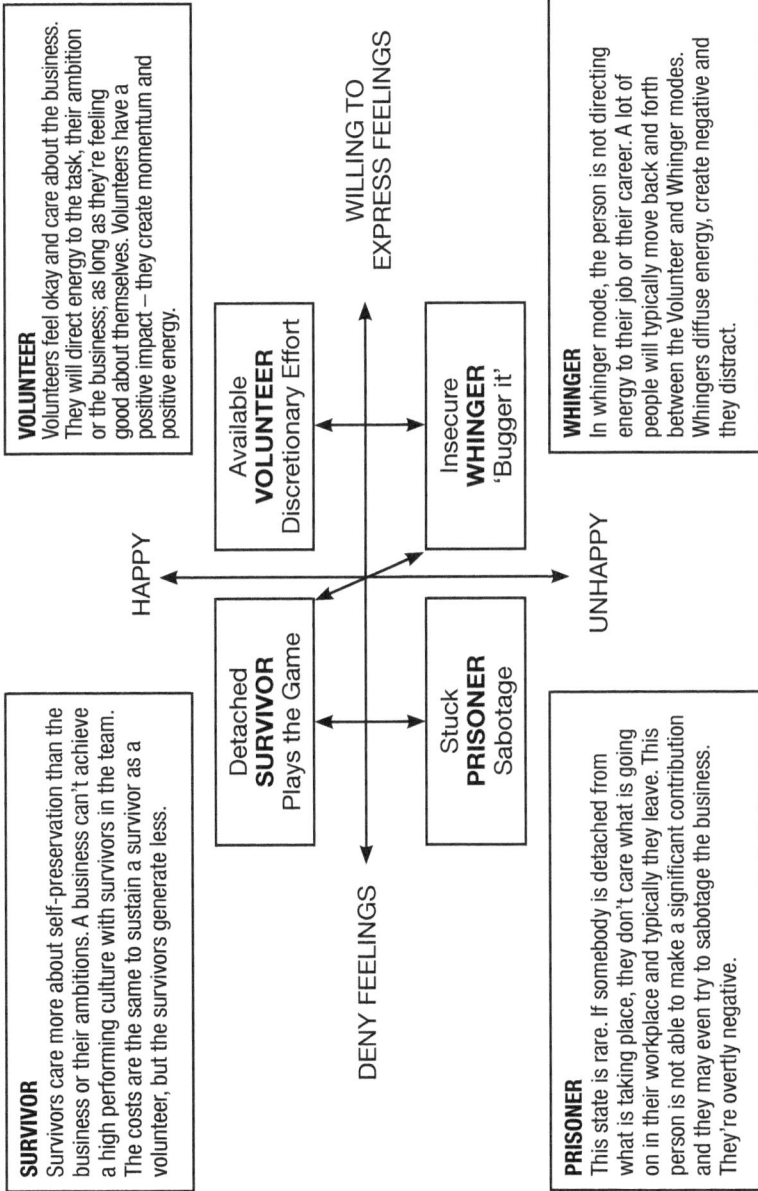

VOLUNTEER
Volunteers feel okay and care about the business. They will direct energy to the task, their ambition or the business; as long as they're feeling good about themselves. Volunteers have a positive impact – they create momentum and positive energy.

SURVIVOR
Survivors care more about self-preservation than the business or their ambitions. A business can't achieve a high performing culture with survivors in the team. The costs are the same to sustain a survivor as a volunteer, but the survivors generate less.

WHINGER
In whinger mode, the person is not directing energy to their job or their career. A lot of people will typically move back and forth between the Volunteer and Whinger modes. Whingers diffuse energy, create negative and they distract.

PRISONER
This state is rare. If somebody is detached from what is taking place, they don't care what is going on in their workplace and typically they leave. This person is not able to make a significant contribution and they may even try to sabotage the business. They're overtly negative.

WILLING TO EXPRESS FEELINGS

DENY FEELINGS

HAPPY

UNHAPPY

Available
VOLUNTEER
Discretionary Effort

Insecure
WHINGER
'Bugger it'

Detached
SURVIVOR
Plays the Game

Stuck
PRISONER
Sabotage

Oz Model of Work Personalities, developed by Dr John Evans and Christina Afors, as part of the Australian Quality Council - Cultural Imprint Study (1994)

The ideal team environment is one where everyone comes to work every single day as a positive Volunteer. However that would be an unrealistic expectation because sometimes, depending on what happens from one moment to the next, we can all shift from one of these personality types to another.

It is also important to resist the temptation to suggest that if someone is not a Volunteer, then it is all negative. On the contrary, a positive of the Whinger personality is the willingness to express themselves so if you want to know what's happening in your business, ask a Whinger.

Watch out for the Survivor as they are more interested in self-preservation than the business or even their own ambitions.

Finally, the Prisoner is so detached from the business they tend to contribute very little and may even directly or indirectly sabotage the business. If this is the case, then it's time to have that hard conversation immediately to determine if they and the situation can be positively changed or if it is better to move them out of your business.

OZ MODEL: WHAT IS YOUR WORKPLACE PERSONALITY PROFILE?

If you would like to gain an insight into your workplace personality and level of happiness (and that of your team), then take these quick five questions. While it's not a scientific study of your true state, the questionnaire could help you determine if you and your business need to take a good hard look at itself. Good luck (and stop laughing as you answer each question as this can be a very helpful tool for your business).

1. When I wake up on work days, I
   a. Jump out of bed, get dressed in my most professional outfit and look forward to the challenging work ahead
   b. Feel generally good about going to work but I dread getting fresh orders from a manager I don't respect and who is giving me a hard time
   c. Go through the motions of getting dressed for work and begin counting down the eight hours until I am home again

d. Roll over and pull the blankets up, knowing I will be half-an-hour late but not caring if I get the sack.

2. When people ask where I work, I
   a. Tell them about the interesting project I am working on and how it might change their lives
   b. Roll my eyes and tell them, adding that it's an OK place to work but the managers/processes/workplace is not up to scratch
   c. Answer with the name only and then change the subject
   d. Tell them but say it's an awful place to work and if I could find another job I'd be out of there quicker than I could say "sack me".

3. When my supervisor asks me into their office, I
   a. Grab a pad, a pen and whatever documents I need and make my way into the meeting with confidence
   b. Become suspicious about what the meeting is about, look over to my workmates and raise my eyebrows, but go into the meeting with all the necessary paperwork
   c. Stand up, go into the office, sit down and tell the manager exactly what they want to hear so I can make the meeting end fast
   d. Tell the manager I can't go and instead go out for a coffee break.

4. When my manager asks me to do a task outside my usual duties, I
   a. Give it a shot as I figure someone has to do it to help out the team
   b. Say I will then talk with workmates to see if they think the request is as out of line as I believe it to be
   c. Ask the manager exactly what they want done and just do that
   d. Tell the manager no, adding that if they compel me, then there will be trouble.

5. When I think about the business, I feel
   a. Happy with what we are trying to achieve and feel part of the team
   b. The job is OK but the way I am asked to do it is all wrong, and everyone who works there knows what I am talking about
   c. Nothing, it's a job and I am doing it to get paid
   d. Hate as I am trapped. If I could leave, I would, but I can't so the bastards will just have to put up with me and I am not going to make it easy for them. *(Sorry for the swearing – please remember this is not my quiz.)*

RESULTS:

Mainly As then you are a Volunteer. You are happy so make it count and guard against negativity.

Mainly Bs then you are a Whinger. Make your whinge count by telling someone who can do something to fix your problems (even if that's you fixing your own behaviour). If you do, you may be on the path to glory once again.

Mainly Cs then you are a Survivor. You are just going through the motions so it's time to decide to act with feeling or remain a workplace drone with a heart of stone. Be a whinger - you will feel better and you may even become a volunteer.

Mainly Ds then you are a Prisoner. Get out and get out now. What's the point of staying at a workplace you despise? Rediscover why you wanted to do this job in the first place and then find another place to do it.

I have seen too many business owners (and their teams) who are Prisoners, Survivors and Whingers; I want to see a lot more Volunteers, and I hope this book helps.

The previous chapter examined the seven mistakes when building a business. Before we look at why your systems may not be working, let me remind you of the seven mistakes to avoid when building your people, your team.

For those of you who haven't yet taken the step of hiring people, remember you are still a team of one so this chapter will be helpful in showing you what not to do once you have grown beyond yourself. For those of you with a team, it will be a good reality check to see if anything needs to be addressed immediately. I encourage you to read these mistakes with a sense of irony to truly embody the key messages I'm imparting.

There are seven main mistakes business owners make when building their People.

MISTAKE #1: YOU WANT ME TO DO WHAT?

You might think staff just love it when they're constantly asked to do more than they believe is their role and responsibilities. *Not.*

This happens because roles and tasks are developed on the fly as the business grows rapidly. As a result, staff members with extra skills (and goodwill) often take on more and more responsibility, initially for no extra money or reward.

Solution: Develop position descriptions (PD) for each role within the business to clearly outline what the position actually does in terms of responsibilities, tasks and delegations before you advertise and undertake a costly recruitment process. This will identify what you are actually looking for in a person and the skills they should have. This will increase the likelihood of you recruiting the right person.

It doesn't matter if your name is in every position on your organisational chart. The sooner you have clarity on the positions in your business, the easier it will be for you to switch hats, become more productive and gain help in the areas you need as your cash flow builds.

MISTAKE #2: JUST GET SOMEONE NOW

Surely a quick recruitment process is ideal. Um, no. There's a big difference between a quick selection process which brings in the ideal candidate who matches the skills you are *actually* seeking rather than simply a warm body to fix the problems. Unfortunately, this often occurs because of no clear PD or urgency. Vacancy situations are the result of a lack of planning to meet expected or increased workload demand, and as you know, lack of planning is setting yourself up to fail.

Solution: Value the recruitment process. Either take your time to determine what attributes and skills you need (PD) and how the ideal person matches the culture and values of your business, or don't do it at all. Spending your valuable time undertaking a 'bogus' recruitment process will just create more work for you and become another problem rather than the solution you were seeking. Also consider your succession planning strategy. You should have a clear plan for when people move on or are promoted. Take the time to pre-empt any people issues you might encounter.

My rant: Please stop wasting people's time by writing a job ad (or outsourcing this to a recruitment agency) that doesn't accurately reflect the position or include the mandatory knowledge, skills and qualifications needed. Nothing annoys candidates more than reading an ad, getting excited and then opening the attached PD to find they don't meet the mandatory qualifications, don't have the necessary experience and can't see a clear correlation between the promising ad and what the job really is (which they also cannot do).

MISTAKE #3: YOU HAVE FREE REIN

Please stop saying this to candidates in their interview because I've yet to see this actually happen. Why? Because at the time of the interview, most business owners haven't yet determined what they want the candidate to do (see mistakes #1 and #2), plus they don't really want to relinquish control of any parts of their business. Free rein can also give the candidate the misconception they don't have to be responsible or accountable for anything.

Result: The new staff member enters your business excited, thinking they're going to change the world by developing a role from scratch yet soon loses interest and energy as they get stifled and disillusioned by continually being told 'no' or 'not yet' or 'let me think about it', and no decision ever eventuates.

Eventually, they will leave you because they're so frustrated and you have to start the process all over again. Instead of embracing the idea that many hands make light work; you're still tired, overworked, angry and maybe disappointed with your staff member who didn't work out. But whose fault was it that the help didn't live up to expectations?

Solution: Stop wasting people's time and energy, and be ready and willing to either embrace help and new ideas or keep struggling on your own, doing the same old thing. Put the time into understanding what you want someone to do and then empower them to do it. This will free you to keep doing the tasks that light you up (and why you started the business in the first place).

MISTAKE #4: IF I TRAIN THEM, THEY'LL LEAVE SO I DON'T

And if you don't train them, they may also leave. Or even worse, they may stay and simply 'exist' in your business, becoming a drain on your finances and energy. If they're not productive, it's probably because you haven't trained them what to do or invested in them.

This is a double-edged sword so the quicker you realise that training is an investment in the long-term success of your business and not an expense, the quicker your business will improve.

My mantra is 'learn something new every day' which means I am always 'in training'. I encourage you to also adopt this approach so it becomes a daily Brick in building your house of knowledge.

Solution: Embrace training because if you invest time and money into ensuring everyone is delivering consistent quality products and services to your clients, your team will help your business grow and build your repeat clients. This solution follows Richard Branson's philosophy 'Train people well enough so they can leave; treat them well enough so they don't want to'.

So who would you prefer: the untrained person who stays and costs you money or the trained person who makes you money and may (or may not) leave?

MISTAKE #5: INDUCTION IS JUST A TOUR OF THE OFFICE

Induction is *not* just a tour of the office, and those business owners who don't develop a comprehensive induction program which informs, trains as well as tests the performance of their new employees, are missing a huge opportunity.

Your investment in induction is equally, if not more, important than the recruitment process. Probation is the time to find out if the new recruit is the right fit for your business and culture, and can apply the knowledge and skills they outlined in their resume and at the interview. Remember however, that while you're assessing the suitability of their fit for you, they're also checking out you and your business to see if they want to stay.

The missing piece, which many business owners forget, is the time it takes for someone new to settle in. In case you haven't taken this step yet or don't know the numbers, here is the reality. It usually takes at least three months, sometimes six, for people to start feeling comfortable, confident and that they belong in this new environment; able to perform to your high standards. Very few people hit the ground running, regardless of what they have told you in an interview to gain the position.

Solution: Support new people and give them time to settle in while progressively reviewing their knowledge, skills, experience and fit with the business. Do this effectively by implementing a structured, documented and regularly monitored induction program.

MISTAKE #6: WHY CAN'T THEY JUST DO IT THE WAY I WANT?

That's easy. Because you haven't documented clearly and simply the system for how things are done at your business. Oh, and they can't read minds.

Solution: Stop assuming people know instinctively what you want them to do. No one can recall everything they're told on day one (or even day seventy-two). Write it down. Help them to help you.

MISTAKE #7: THAT DOESN'T APPLY TO THEM BECAUSE …

This is all about consciously or subconsciously playing favourites with some staff because you value one or more of them above the others. Maybe they've been with you the longest, or you think you can't do certain work without them or they are family members. Whatever the reason, playing favourites doesn't work.

Having different rules for different people, without any explanation or transparency, is the quickest way to cause division and disharmony within a team, and will probably result in you eventually losing very good people (often not your favourites).

Staff will quickly know if you let someone get away with something. Those to whom you're giving special treatment will also be quick to see the difference and could use this as a bargaining chip against you. Put yourself in the non-favourite's shoes: how would you feel?

Solution: Stop playing favourites. If there's a valid reason for doing so (and that's a big if), get it out in the open so everyone can acknowledge it and move on. Your

> Be comfortable having the hard conversation … with yourself and your team

staff will understand if you explain; otherwise they will gossip, usually in a negative way. Set yourself up for success and explain your reasons.

GENEROSITY CAN BE A CURSE

One of my clients took all his staff and their partners to a local restaurant for an all-expenses paid celebratory Christmas dinner and I was honoured to be invited. However, I was appalled to see a few staff members taking advantage of this generosity by ordering cocktails and top-shelf spirits rather than standard drinks.

This occurred in part because the business owner didn't set boundaries, but they also allowed the behaviour to continue. It's disappointing to think there's a need to outline the rules to adults at a private function, but alas, it is essential because it cannot and should not be assumed that everyone knows what is appropriate behaviour.

Solution

Don't let staff take advantage of you because you want to be seen as a nice boss and their friend. Be generous for sure, and that's wonderful. But set clear boundaries upfront so staff don't take unexpected liberties such as leaving the office to 'work from home' without having permission to do this.

Open plan offices may not be the answer

This did seem like a good idea a few years ago, but research is now proving that taking into account illness, productivity and optimum working styles; open plan is not the ideal option it was once thought to be.

In 2013, Richard de Dear and colleague Jungsoo Kim reviewed 42,000 responses in a post-occupancy survey and discovered people in open plan offices were far less satisfied with their workplace environment than people in enclosed offices with doors. Being close to colleagues did have some benefits for those who got their energy from others, but the introverted workers were overwhelmed by the increased noise and reduction in privacy. They also found it difficult to work when they could hear other people talking.

This research is supported by Queensland University of Technology's Institute of Health and Biomedical Innovation researcher Vinesh Oommen, who found 'in 90% of the responses, open plan offices were causing high levels of conflict, blood pressure and staff turnover. The high level of noise causes employees to lose concentration, leading to low productivity; there are privacy issues because everyone can see what you're doing on the computer or hear what you're saying on the phone; and there is a feeling of insecurity'.

The numbers also support the negative aspects of open plan offices:

- 95 percent of workers say working privately is important to them
  Source: Steelcase research

- 62 percent of extra sick days are taken in open-plan offices
  Source: *Scandinavian Journal of Work, Environment & Health*, 2011

I have observed similar phenomena in many businesses because the reality is not everyone works in the same way. Some people, like me, do not work well in silence and often have noise, usually music, on in the background to get into their groove. For others, it's the complete opposite and hearing other people's conversations drives them batty, making them lose concentration which lowers their productivity.

Also, not everyone wants to be everyone else's friend at work nor do they want to socialise outside of work hours. And it's not necessarily because they don't want to be part of a team. Many people who fall into this category respect, tolerate and get along with their colleagues; but for them, work is work. Their life outside of work is personal and private, and it shouldn't be viewed as a negative simply because they don't want to 'share'.

<u>Solution:</u> It's all a question of balance because a one size fits all approach to an office doesn't work. Therefore, find out what environment everyone needs (including you) to work at their best and come up with a happy and fair compromise.

Building your business ..... one brick at a time

1. What are your top three People Wolves?

2. What is one thing you need to change about each Wolf to keep it at bay?

3. When will you start to make this change?

My People Wolf is ...	What is 1 thing I need to change to keep these Wolves at bay?	I will start making this change ...
Example	Expectations	Review position descriptions to ensure they accurately reflect the required tasks of the position	Tomorrow
People Wolf 1			
People Wolf 2			
People Wolf 3			

Now you know the Business and People mistakes in your BPS Roadmap, let's look at the Systems mistakes to determine what's really costing your business time and money.

Chapter 11

Systems
Shh ... Don't Mention the 'S' word

People come and go but the systems remain.

Michael Gerber

ention the words 'policy' or 'procedures' and most people either cringe or roll their eyes. I wonder if this is also your reaction to these words?'

When I mention 'systems' to a business owner, the responses are predictable:

- 'I need them but ...'
- 'I wish I had them but ...'
- 'I know I need them but ...'

- 'I've read *The E-Myth* and get the importance and value of systems but …'

The 'but' is often followed by one of several responses:

- '… I'm too busy'
- '… I don't have time'
- '… we've got them and they don't work'
- '… we've got them and no one uses them'

I started to wonder why this was the case. Why is it that most business owners know they need systems to have a profitable, productive, scalable and saleable business but few have actually taken the next step to implement this (or implement it fully)?

Then I figured it out. There are three main reasons why businesses don't invest the time and money to build simple systems:

1. They believe that they and their staff can and should be doing it themselves

2. They don't know how to build simple systems (not really)

3. They don't know where to start (and still keep bringing in the cash)

All of these reasons are valid and true so which one resonates best with you?

Consider one of the best systemised businesses ever developed: McDonald's is a business run by fifteen year olds and it operates like clockwork because every task and customer service script is documented so it can be easily learned and followed. But do you really think McDonald's built their systems themselves?

Everyone needs help to get things done, in life and in business. Why? Because we're all too close to what we do. Most of us need help to tease out the steps we undertake through habit and instinct, and turn this information into simple user-friendly systems.

Even as a business systems specialist, I give my work to others, not only to check for typos but also to ensure it's simple and easy to follow.

To further demonstrate this point, here are seven mistakes to avoid when building the Systems on your BPS Roadmap.

MISTAKE #1: BELIEVING YOU AND YOUR TEAM HAVE THE EXPERTISE TO DO THIS

In my twenty years of experience, it has been very rare for me to find someone in a business who can extract the step-by-step information out of the heads of the owner and every team member that explains exactly how they do their jobs, and then turn that information into simple procedures and templates.

Think about your Business: Does anyone have this skill and expertise ... really?

If your answer is yes – here's my next question:

Are you giving that person (which may be you) the time and space needed to develop your business' simple procedures, or are you like most business owners who say to their staff: "As part of your work, document what you do as you go".

If you say this to your team or yourself, please know IT DOESN'T HAPPEN.

Unless people are pulled offline or allocated specific time outside their current tasks, but in work time, it won't get done. People are too busy serving that client, dealing with paperwork, delivering that training etc. to stop and think about what they just did and then document it simply and easily for everyone to follow.

MISTAKE #2: WAITING UNTIL YOUR BUSINESS IS SLOW BEFORE YOU START

Not having documented policies and procedures is costing you time and money *now*.

Reality: There is never a good time to start building your systems. But the longer you wait, the higher the risk will be that this knowledge will walk out the door. So get over it and start documenting today.

MISTAKE #3: BUILDING SYSTEMS AROUND PEOPLE AND NOT POSITIONS

It's great when people start documenting what they do. However, unless the process is aligned to a key position within the business, chances are you will only get their perspective (which may include their bad habits) on how they do it rather than how you believe it should be done.

MISTAKE #4: REMAINING IN DRAFT MODE

Rather than working on Pareto's 80–20 rule and letting the procedures loose to test in the 'real' business, the systems never get released because people say they're still working on them or checking them. This means the business and the team remain in a constant state of 'Are we there yet?' and feel like no progress has been made, and probably never will be.

MISTAKE #5: CONSTANT CHANGES

This is the opposite extreme from Mistake #5 where every system or process is constantly tweaked and updated so you're up to version twenty-two in the first week. It's great to get feedback and ideas so I suggest capturing and reviewing those ideas. Ask if the issue is costing you time and money *right now*. If it is, fix it immediately. If not, review it on a monthly basis to see if the issue has either resolved itself or still needs to be addressed.

MISTAKE #6: ALL TEXT – NO FLOWCHARTS OR TEMPLATES

Many systems are never implemented because there are simply too many words. They either don't make sense, are riddled with jargon or need to be read three times before anyone has any idea of what has been said. People generally learn in four different ways: visually, aurally, by reading and writing or kinaesthetically (VARK). Implement systems that encompass these different learning styles to ensure they will be used rather than left sitting on the shelf (or in the hidden file directory) gathering dust.

MISTAKE #7: SYSTEMS EQUAL CHANGE

Tony Robbins said, 'Change is inevitable, progress is optional.' You can write the best systems and procedures in the world and think the job is done. However, if you don't address past implementation issues and build change management, ownership and training into your systems implementation strategy; it's bound to fail.

Most people want clarity and structure in their work because once they have them, freedom, initiative and creativity flow. Why? Continuous improvement and new ideas are encouraged and therefore become embedded in the culture. When you see these signs of change, you'll know the business can operate without you and your team being available 24/7.

At this point you will know whether you have built your Systems Roadmap for a simple, profitable business you love. If not, which of these seven mistakes do you need to review to start building your solid foundations?

If you have implemented great systems, pulled the knowledge out of people's heads, documented it into easy to follow procedures

> Don't blame the system when things go wrong or not according to plan - find out WHY

and information, integrated the change management process as part of development and implementation so everyone is on board and people are <u>still</u> not following your processes; then this is happening for one of two reasons:

1. Your people need more training.

2. Your people (including you) are making a choice not to follow the processes. This is a performance issue you need to address immediately.

SYSTEMS ARE FOR EVERYONE

I worked with a particular client for nearly six months, and in that time, we captured all the knowledge of his business from his head and his nine staff and documented this information into simple systems: step-by-step procedures, flowcharts, checklists and templates. I also helped address unacceptable behaviours and bad habits as part of the change management process.

Things were going well. The staff's expectations were now very clear, backup plans were in place and everyone was playing their part. Or so I thought.

About a month after full implementation, I walked in and felt a negative change in the air. The place was very quiet and there wasn't as much camaraderie as usual. After a few informal chats with staff members, who were very guarded in their responses, I pulled the Business Manager aside and asked what had happened.

She told me the owner had gone back to his old ways of skipping processes and changing the order of jobs in the queue. This was his modus operandi to respond to demands from his 'mates rates' clients who wanted speedy service for a substantially reduced rate.

By constantly changing the priority order of work, based on which client rang that day rather than completing specific processes, several things were being repeated:

- Increased mistakes
- Decreased quality of work
- Things were being missed
- Confusion was rampant
- Staff felt disillusioned and disempowered ... again

In one month, the business had gone from one with happy staff who finally knew and agreed on the tasks everyone completed in their specific roles, and how each part fitted into the bigger jigsaw; to a business filled with chaos, discontent and a feeling that nothing had changed after all.

Why? The owner had decided he was above the systems and processes he had desperately wanted my help to develop so, as he told me, 'staff could toe the line and do things properly'.

Systems work brilliantly when everyone follows them including those at the top. Unfortunately, as this business owner didn't lead by example, all the good work I had undertaken within his business was undone in an instant.

Solution

Value the investment in the process: it works. Developing systems can feel like you're taking two steps forward, six back, but this is normal. Keep going. It's simply part of the process you have to go through to achieve success. As CS Lewis said: 'Isn't it funny how day by day nothing changes, but when you look back everything is different.'

Building your business ..... one brick at a time

1. What are your top three Systems Wolves?

2. What is one thing you need to change about each Wolf to keep it at bay?

3. When will you actually make this change?

	My Systems Wolf is ...	What is 1 thing I need to change to keep these Wolves at bay?	I will start making this change ...
Example	Procrastination	Develop your organisational chart and start documenting the procedures for each position	Tomorrow
Systems Wolf 1			
Systems Wolf 2			
Systems Wolf 3			

You should now be clear about what you shouldn't do as you build your BPS Roadmap for a simple, profitable business you love. Now it's time to look at the simple solutions to help you build a CLEAR BPS Roadmap for an even better business.

Chapter 12

Get CLEAR on Your BPS Roadmap

Why do I stand up here? I stand upon my desk to remind myself
that we must constantly look at things in a different way.

John Keating, Dead Poets Society

I apologise if you have arrived at this page and are feeling a little angry, anxious or ready to throw your hands in the air and chuck it all in. But wait, because it's now time for the good stuff.

Up to this point, I have highlighted some of the mistakes you may have made in building your BPS Roadmap. Now it's time for … wait for it … *solutions*. Yes, the rest of the book is about simple strategies that will help you build the simple, profitable business you have always desired.

To finish this part of the book, I will outline my five step process to get you CLEAR on what I call 'Building your BPS Roadmap' which will help you take your business from where you are now to where you want to be.

Why a five step process? Well, after working with countless business owners I realised in order to go from confusion, frustration and feeling overwhelmed to the desired state of peace of mind, owners needed a way to separate the woods from the trees. This can be very difficult if you don't know where to start or even what first small step to take.

The five step acronym I have developed to build the BPS Roadmap is **CLEAR**:

Clarity
Leadership
Establish
Analysis
Reality

Within each of these five steps, there are a number of signposts to work through as you build your BPS Roadmap to your ultimate business house. And once you have a CLEAR roadmap, the next steps are simple.

5 Steps to Build your BPS Roadmap

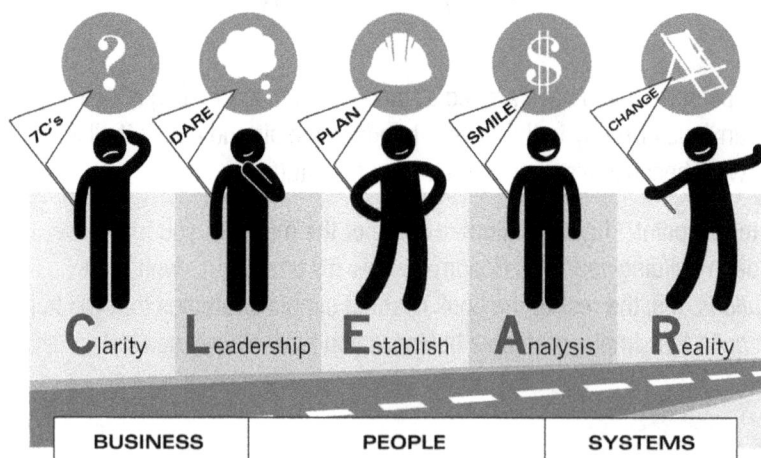

IT'S EASIER THAN YOU THINK

One of my clients had a great business with ten fantastic staff but he was exhausted and fed up for several reasons:

- Turnover was great but profit and cash flow weren't at the levels he wanted

- He was spending most of his day dealing with staff, even though there were two team leaders who were supposed to do that

- He was constantly fixing mistakes or putting out fires because even though he had great designers, he couldn't trust them to send plans to clients without his once-over

The client engaged me through my retainer package, and once onsite I implemented my five step CLEAR process to build his BPS Roadmap.

Once he had completed the five steps, the many outcomes he gained in his BPS included:

- Clarity about where his business was NOW and where he wanted to take it in the FUTURE

- Implemented a new business model and organisational structures

- Redefined roles and position descriptions to more accurately reflect the scope of the work

- Addressed unacceptable behaviours and reset boundaries and expectations

- Documented procedures for all positions across the business

- Simplified or removed duplicated processes

The ultimate result was that, once again, my client had a business he loved because:

- Staff knew what to do and weren't constantly annoying him with inane questions.

- Clients were receiving a consistent and quality experience, every time.

- He had time and money to do what he wanted including taking holidays without contacting the office.

- His wife was able to reduce her working hours in the business to part time which she loved.

One day I asked him why he had hired me, and he said, 'I knew you'd worked with other building designers so you understood the jargon and the industry. I didn't know what was wrong in my business or how you'd solve it, but after talking to you, I knew you'd help my business and you did.'

This example illustrates the power of my five step CLEAR process.

Want to hear more?

Building your business .....
one brick at a time

1. What are your top three BPS Wolves?

2. What is one thing you need to change about each Wolf to keep
it at bay?

3. When will you start to make this change?

	My BPS Wolf is ...	What is 1 thing I need to change to keep these Wolves at bay?	I will start making this change ...
Example	*Procrastination*	*Develop Weekly Rituals including morning and evening tasks I will do every day*	*Tomorrow*
BPS Wolf 1			
BPS Wolf 2			
BPS Wolf 3			

The first step in building your BPS Roadmap is Clarity which is often
the one thing many business owners lack. Now let me show you how
gaining CLARITY in your BPS stops you feeling confused, frustrated and
overwhelmed.

Chapter 13

CLARITY
The Seven Cs

Clarity

If you can't explain it simply, you don't understand it enough.

Albert Einstein

ow much do you crave *Clarity* in your business and your life? Is this something you have achieved or are you still searching through the fog, hoping one day the light will break through and it will all make sense? Let me help you with this.

Clarity is defined as clearness, the quality of being coherent and easily understood. For me, that's like the *'How's the serenity?'* moment in the Australian movie *The Castle.*

What does clarity mean to you? When I talk to small business owners, clarity for them usually means just one thing: knowing what to do next. This is a place to start but not always the best place because more often than not, focusing on the next step means one of two things:

1. You keep jumping from task to task because you're uncertain about the path you should be taking.

2. You're so overwhelmed by everything you have to do that you can't see the wood for the trees; so you stop *everything* because what you're doing isn't working.

These things are happening because without clarity about what they do, who they work with, why they do what they do, how they're different from their competitors and what they want to achieve in the coming year, they can't expect their potential clients to jump onboard and become their money train. Anyone in this place, spinning their wheels and going nowhere (and it's a place I've been in more than once), needs clarity to give them focus and momentum to build their business in a different way.

But clarity is much more than just focus. I don't know about you but unless I'm clear on what I'm doing and the direction I need to take my business, I usually get stuck.

Result: I procrastinate and get distracted by shiny objects so I spend my time and energy doing lots of things but achieving very little. Have you been in this place?

My extensive work portfolio has led me to understand that clarity has seven components, which I call **The Seven Cs**. By addressing these seven areas, I can move business owners from a state of frustration and feeling overwhelmed to a place of clarity, calmness and real change.

Although it does take time to achieve Clarity (as with anything that is worthwhile doing), you'll know when you're there because:

- you and your team love to come to work
- everyone knows what they're doing
- your clients are receiving a consistently high quality product and experience which meets their needs
- you can spend time building your dream business and doing the work you love *and*
- you can take guilt-free holidays.

Doesn't that sound great? Isn't this why you took the brave step to go out on your own and establish your business in the first place? Clarity is always needed, no matter which type of business you have built: Straw, Stick, Brick or The Reno. And clarity is needed *urgently* for The Rundown business.

Now you've decided to change the way you're running your business, let me help you get clarity on what has to be done to make it happen *now*.

I will examine a few of The Seven C's simultaneously rather than dealing with each one individually, but all are critical to building a better business. Clarity is the key to unlocking the hidden potential in your BPS, but it can be hard to gain clarity when you don't know how to proceed.

By understanding and examining my experiences with clients and colleagues, I discovered clarity is about addressing seven key areas:

1. **Core**
2. **Customers**
3. **Cash**
4. **Culture**
5. **Context**

6. **Capacity**
7. **Capability**

Let's look at what each of these areas means because unless you gain clarity in each one, it won't be possible to build the simple, profitable business you love. It also means you can't be assured you actually have a Brick business which will not be blown down by the Wolf.

Core

Core is about understanding and being able to clearly articulate the specifics of your business. Although this sounds very easy, it can be one of the hardest things to determine. There are certain things you need to be able to articulate clearly:

- What you do
- How you do it
- The products and services you offer
- The problems you solve
- The solutions you provide
- How you are different to your competitors
- Why you do what you do

If you can't rattle off your responses to these points quickly and easily, how can you expect clients to find you and engage you to help their business? It would be near impossible. Without clarity about your core business, how can you expect your team to be on the same page?

And, most importantly, if you're not clear on your core business, you can't build your BPS Roadmap. Instead, you may end up wasting time developing processes for products and services you'll no longer be offering. This is why it's so important to determine what's really costing you and your business time and money. Is it your business model or your systems? Clarity on your *core* means time and energy are not wasted.

As I mentioned earlier, when talking about whether you have a business or a hobby, often the reason an owner remains in business is because they are passionate about something. Maybe it's the product they sell or maybe it's having the independence of business ownership. There could be many reasons.

There is a lot of commentary in the business world that says until you know your *why*, you won't be truly successful in business. This idea is further cemented by the exceptional TED talk by Simon Sinek, who says, 'People don't buy what you do, people buy why you do what you do.'

I don't know about you but I have struggled for a long time to determine my *why*. I have read lots of books and listened to many successful business people talking about the need for passion and having a strong *why* – the driver for their success. The thing I've found interesting is while most people talk about the importance of discovering your *why*, they haven't told me *how* to discover it beyond some generic ideas like 'find out what really makes you happy and do that'. Well, if I'm honest, I'm happiest when I'm living and breathing sport particularly Hawthorn (AFL) and netball, but I don't believe that's why I'm in business. However, when I dig a bit deeper, what I love about sport is the synchronicity of teams playing together, following the system, as one living breathing being … the same as teams of people in businesses, working together as one. It's like an orchestra; completely different instruments all playing different parts of the symphony at different and/or at simultaneous times but somehow all working together to play the most majestic and glorious music only angels could have created.

What I've discovered is that my *why*, beyond that of making a difference like many business owners, is making sense of things especially if they're complicated. And I gained this lightbulb moment when I read Ridgely Goldsborough's book *The Why Engine*. Goldsborough describes the nine different *whys* and provides the system to determine which why is your primary driver.

Although I connected with a number of them, the best one for me described people who make sense of things and find it impossible to NOT solve other people's problems. And that is me to a T. I have now embraced my deeper *why* (which was always there; I just hadn't formalised it into words) and integrated it into my tagline, my products and my services because I'm all about solving small business problems with simple solutions.

So what's your *WHY*? Why are you still in business (and please don't say to make money because that's a given for anyone who starts and runs a business)?

Core is the blueprint of your business, just like the plans of your house. If it's a service station then your core is fuel, milk and access to clean toilets. If you're a building designer, your core might be commercial dwellings. It doesn't mean you don't undertake other work; it's all about where you focus your time and energy to gain the best return on your effort.

Your core is also what you are known for – it is your primary focus. For instance, you are a vet who specialises in treating birds rather than a general practice vet. You are an accountant for small businesses rather than large corporations. You are an electrical company specialising in new home installation.

Your core provides the focus for where your primary income is derived. It is not your product. Product is an outcome of understanding your core. Product is the offering that stems from your core. Knowing what your core is assists in recruiting people (those who only want to work for small businesses) and building systems (they need to be versatile and flexible to meet the diversity of clients) and so on.

Now you have some insight into determining what your core is, ask yourself what your business is *really*. What is your *why*? And how can you articulate that clearly so potential clients want to deal with you and are willing to pay?

Clients

Once you have clarity on what your business Core is all about, the next step is to gain clarity regarding your **Clients**. Again, this can be a difficult thing to determine. Maybe your services could be relevant for many industry sectors rather than occupy a specific niche. If you can't clearly articulate who are your ideal clients, it can mean your precious time is spent with the wrong ones. And wrong clients mean low income and an unhappy business owner.

How to identify the wrong client:

- Anyone shopping around on price
- Anyone who doesn't share your values and business ethics
- Anyone who doesn't have the budget, or desire, to part with money to engage your services

If you cannot identify your ideal client, you risk being everything to everyone and master of nothing. This is a very hard sell.

Clients constitute one of my more challenging C's so I'm going to share my experiences with you in the hope it will help you gain clarity with your own clients.

Clients have been a challenge for me because I have experience in over thirteen industry sectors including vocational education and training (VET), building design, audit and volunteer management. As an innovative problem solver, I also love learning about new industries and businesses so specialising in one industry sector doesn't bring out the best in me nor does it make me happy.

Rather than specialising in one industry sector such as building designers, I have discovered I have two very specific areas of interest: one is based on the size of a business and the problems facing the owners; and the second is working with registered training organisations (RTOs).

As a Speaker, Author and Troubleshooter, I specialise in helping business owners build their BPS Roadmap for the simple, profitable business they love. Generally, these owners have between five and twenty staff and the owner is frustrated for several reasons. They know there's something wrong with the business but they don't know what it is or how to fix it. Also, they want to grow or improve their business but are not sure where to start.

I can and do work with businesses which sit outside these two areas of interest – *if* the owner is the type of person I want to work with. Not everyone can and should be my client, just as you could not expect to have everyone as your client either.

Business owners with whom I'm happy to work:

- Know something needs to change in their business for the better, now and in the future.
- Value an external perspective and are open to new and sometimes challenging ideas.
- Are willing to invest time and money in improving and growing their business.
- Can accept criticism and accept responsibility for their own possible contribution to the current state of the business, both good and bad.

Have you determined specifically your ideal client, taking into account their values and the industry sector in which they work? Who do you want to work with and, equally important, who do you *not* want to work with? It's important to ensure you are spending your time with quality people who value you and what you do – and have the ability to pay.

Cash

Like many, I have been guilty of running a hobby rather than a profitable business mainly because I've wanted to help people. Does this sound like you, too? But helpfulness and goodwill don't pay the bills, although I wish they did. And they don't keep the doors open, pay the mortgage or, in the worst cases, save relationships, kids or the health of many business owners. Unfortunately I have seen this situation too often, and it can quickly become the story for many business owners rather than being a rare occurrence.

How does this happen? Why don't owners see the warning signs much earlier and address the problems so their businesses don't revert to Straw or even The Rundown that will be demolished as soon as they close their doors?

Many of these situations are the result of a multitude of factors which, when combined, often result in disaster:

- No understanding of the financial numbers within the business: why they're important, what to look at and when, and failing to undertake professional development to gain this understanding

- Lack of interest in the financial numbers which have been ignored or dismissed outright, and the right assistance hasn't been engaged

- No comprehension of how much it actually costs to run the business which is beyond the expenses that appear on the profit and loss statement

- No appreciation that time is money, and this has not been factored into any planning or cost-recovery modelling

- Belief it will eventually turn around but there is no clear strategy to do this (including lead generation) and the business is being run on hope

- Lack of recognition that not every idea for a business will generate income through products or services

- No knowledge of the difference between turnover, cash flow and profit

- Belief the business is profitable if there's money in the bank

What does this all mean? Cash flow or **money** is king, and if you want a profitable business, at a minimum you need to determine how much money you need to cover costs each month. Once you have covered costs, you can then increase sales to go from breaking even to making a profit. Once you are making a profit, you can invest back into the business to take it to the next level or maybe go on that much needed holiday. Cash in the bank does not mean cash in your pocket.

To track my numbers quickly and easily, I have an Excel spreadsheet which shows me budgeted and actual expenses as well as money coming in each month against three categories: possible, work in progress and invoiced.

I encourage you to develop your own tracking system so you can run a profitable business rather than a hobby. Know your numbers and watch them every day. Seek help with this if you want to turn your business around.

Remember: No money means no business.

Culture

Culture is another aspect you need to determine for your business. Often it's something that evolves by itself, over time, rather than being something fostered by you, the business owner. Culture is part of what makes your business different from your competitors and why people want to work for you rather than someone else. It builds on your value as the owner and helps define boundaries and expectations.

The culture of a business can be defined by a few key criteria:

- Formal or informal (dress, language, written, verbal)
- Laidback and casual
- Corporate
- Bureaucratic

- Family friendly
- Flexible
- Rigid
- Bright and colourful
- What some may see as boring

Once you have determined the culture of your business, this needs to be accurately and consistently reflected throughout your business including:

- Branding and messaging including website colours, font and logo
- Management style
- Liaison with clients and team
- Business systems and documentation

> Clarity, consistency and congruence go hand in hand

So is your business culture clear to you, your team and your clients or is there a disconnect you need to address?

Context

When I'm working with anyone to solve a problem, the most important thing I keep in mind is the **context** of the situation. Rather than jumping to conclusions based on assumptions, I endeavour to ask as many questions as I need to get below the surface to the real cause of the problem.

Too often, I see people reacting to situations without knowing all the facts or understanding the interconnected circumstances that may have led up to the current event. This leads to a quick fix which will only mask and not solve the problem.

It is very important to gain clarity on the context of situations, problems and opportunities. Otherwise, if you base your decisions on information at face value without also taking into account the actual context, you may be headed for a fall you could have easily avoided by taking the time to ask more questions.

Capability and Capacity

These two C's go hand in hand but are often examined separately or not at all. Think of the times you've brainstormed every outcome you wanted to achieve in a year, in other words, the information documented in your annual business plan. Was any of it actually achieved? If not, was it because you didn't have the **capacity** to complete these additional outcomes on top of your existing workload? Or was it because you didn't have the **capability**?

Instead of setting unrealistic demands on yourself and your staff, ensure you gain clarity on what outcomes are realistic and achievable, taking into account current capability and capacity. Otherwise you will have more disillusionment, feelings of being overwhelmed and frustration.

If these outcomes are important to you, but out of your reach because of lack of capability or capacity, you can make choices: you could obtain additional help if you have the financial means to do so, now or in a month, three months, a year; or you could put some ideas on hold until you're in a more financially viable position.

Remember: Saying yes to everything can lead to disappointment, blame, anxiety and lost clients rather than the desired reward of a simple, profitable business you love.

| Q | Building your business .....
one brick at a time |

1. What are your top three Clarity Wolves?

2. What is one thing you need to change about each Wolf to keep it at bay?

3. When will you start to make this change?

My Clarity Wolf is ...	What is 1 thing I need to change to keep these Wolves at bay?	I will start making this change ...
Example	Clients	Classify my A, B and C business clients	Tomorrow
Clarity Wolf 1			
Clarity Wolf 2			
Clarity Wolf 3			

Now you have Clarity in The Seven C's, it's time to see if you DARE to Lead.

Chapter 14

Do You DARE to Lead?

If your actions inspire others to dream more, lead more,
do more and become more, you are a leader.

John Quincy Adams

The second step to building your BPS Roadmap is all about *Leadership* and whether you **DARE** to be the Leader. The key to this step is recognising that everyone in your business, regardless of their position, should view themselves as a leader and act accordingly. The only variables are the level of responsibility and the decision making parameters. Encourage every person in your business to demonstrate their leadership potential by:

- Looking for ways to improve
- Being the best they can be
- Offering clients amazing service with every connection, no matter how small
- Thinking of new and different products and services
- Being encouraging and supportive
- Being willing to help out

Do you encourage and model this form of leadership in your business so your team can demonstrate their leadership to you, and vice versa?

Within this step, there are four signposts within the acronym **DARE**:

- **D**irection
- **A**ccountability
- **R**esponsibility
- **E**xample

Direction

Unfortunately many business owners fall down in *Leadership* because they want to be everyone's friend and a great boss; and they forget leadership begins with **direction**.

What direction is your business taking? Do you have a clear vision which makes sense to you, your clients and your team? Can anyone refer you to potential clients because the results a client will receive by working with you are clear? Is there a documented plan for this month, this year, and for the following year that builds on the direction you wish to take your business? Are you presenting an image of credibility and expertise to the world? Do you need to change the direction of your business due to market shifts, the economy, legislation changes, technology or innovation?

Accountability

Unfortunately I see too many people missing the **accountability** signpost. Mistakes happen. As I say to my girls in the junior netball team I coach, 'Stuff happens. It's about what you do next that matters.' If they have had an uh-oh moment because they missed a shot or threw away a pass, I need them to quickly refocus, switch back on and get the ball back.

When I take this same philosophy into the business world, unfortunately what I observe these days is too many business owners and their staff spending energy blaming one another or not addressing the issue of accountability at all. Is this what you see as well? And now for the really hard question: do you see this happening in your own business or is it just something that happens in other people's backyards?

Stuff happens so we need to own it. Focus on what you can do to improve and avoid the mistake next time. It will be a much better use of your energy and time than playing the blame game.

Responsibility

This goes hand in hand with Accountability. I get frustrated when people don't take **responsibility** for their own work and own decisions, and the subsequent consequences. In this age of technology, it seems people have lost the art of remembering to do the things they said they would do. Instead of this responsible behaviour, the trend I'm seeing involves excuses like, 'You didn't send me a text message reminder,' or 'You didn't send me an email about that,' even when both people were at the meeting taking notes.

Example

When everyone is a leader in your business, then everyone will step up and be responsible for managing their workload and commitments. If they need help, are you providing guidance, and if need be, some time management training or are you leaving them floundering? Otherwise, what's the point of staff and what's the value of 'your word and promises' to clients?

Key questions for you and your staff to ask:

- What type of leader am I now?

- What type of leader do I want to be?

- How do members of my team lead?

We all know great leaders walk the talk and empower their staff so what's your leadership **example**? I'm sure you have your own way of describing leadership but a simple definition is 'the activity of leading a group of people or an organisation'.

This is where it can get difficult particularly because many business owners are great technicians in their industry or field of

> Fixing other people's mistakes without telling them doesn't teach them the much needed traits of Accountability and Responsibility

expertise but are not always the best leaders in their business. Why? Because they don't want to have the hard conversations with staff (or themselves), and deal directly with the issues and problems. Doing this means you need to **DARE** to lead and demonstrate leadership in everything you do.

WANT A SIMPLE AND EASY WAY TO GROW WITHOUT LOSING YOUR CULTURE?

Look at 15five – http://www.15five.com/ – a simple way to keep everyone aligned with the values and vision of your business, no matter how far or fast you grow.

How 15five works:

- Team members take 15 minutes a week to answer simple questions

- Managers take 5 minutes to engage and provide feedback

- Conversations transform into meaningful action

From little things big things grow which can work both positively and negatively. Avoiding issues and thinking they will either go away or resolve themselves can make the situation worse. You probably know this already so you need to consider what the reasons are if this is still happening. If you want to be a great leader, you have to **DARE** and action it into existence.

Building your business ..... one brick at a time

1. What are your top three Leadership Wolves?

2. What is one thing you need to change about each Wolf to keep it at bay?

3. When will you start to make this change?

	My Leadership Wolf is ...	What is 1 thing I need to change to keep these Wolves at bay?	I will start making this change ...
Example	Playing favourites	Reset boundaries and expectations	Tomorrow
Leadership Wolf 1			
Leadership Wolf 2			
Leadership Wolf 3			

Now you have DARED to Lead, it's time to Establish your PLAN.

Chapter 15

Establish the PLAN

Do not worry if you have built your castles in the air.
They are where they should be.
Now put the foundations under them.
Henry David Thoreau

The third step in the five steps to building your BPS Roadmap is to *Establish* the **PLAN**. In an ideal world, most Reluctant Business Owners would have a plan of some sort, either for the business in general or for the day ahead. But in my experience many owners don't even have a plan in their head, let alone one that's written down, tracked and measured.

You may have heard the saying, 'If you fail to plan then you plan to fail,' which is absolutely true. Where is your own plan: in your head or written down so everyone can see and action it? In order to get clear on your BPS, consider looking at your plan in a slightly different way.

The acronym **PLAN** encompasses four things to consider before developing an Annual Business Plan and moving forward:

- **Past**
- **Landscape**
- **Attitude**
- **Numbers**

If you want to do things differently, you have to address these aspects head on to shift the way you think about them and deal with them. If you don't,

> Learn from the past but don't stay there

you'll continue to repeat the mistakes of the past and remain the Reluctant Business Owner rather than owning the title of 'Business Owner' who has a simple, profitable business you love.

Past

Unfortunately, all too often when I work with business owners to make changes, I come up against a situation where the staff has been through the process many times before and are 'over it'.

These are the most common responses I hear:

- 'Oh yeah, here we go again.'
- 'Been here before, what's going to be different this time?'
- 'Nothing will change.'
- 'We're just going through the motions.'

To allay these fears for your staff, it's essential to look at the **past**. Take the good things which worked then draw a line in the sand so you can shift the organisation or business focus properly. To do this effectively, you need a new approach.

When I talk about the past with my clients, I often conduct what I call my *Past Workshop*. This involves individually interviewing the business owner and the staff, asking them what's happening to gain the true picture of the business.

History tells me the business owner will likely tell me one thing and the staff another, and rightly so because they come from very different perspectives. Owners and staff will never be completely on the same page because the owner has a vested financial interest in the success of the business whereas staff do not. This doesn't mean your people don't want to be there or work hard; it's simply that the motivational drivers are different.

I remember a client saying to me, 'I can't understand why they don't love my business as much as me.' My response, after a pause and a roll of the eyes, was, 'Because it's not their business. They get to come here, do eight hours of great work, leave and get paid, regardless of anything else happening in the business.'

And isn't that exactly what you want them to do or do you have a very unrealistic expectation which needs to shift? As much as possible, you want everyone singing from the same song sheet.

To ensure the success of this process, I ask the owner and/or their staff these questions:

- What is your role? What do you actually do?
- What work do you like to do?
- What work don't you like to do?
- If you were the owner, what three things would you change?
- What has been done before that hasn't worked, and why not?

The answers invariably provide me with an insight into what's happening in the business, both on the surface and bubbling away below.

It's also important in this process to remember that everyone's opinion is valuable. Amazing insights and innovation can be gleaned from anyone in your business, from the administration staff all the way through to management. The answers are there: you just have to ask for them.

In order for this process to be successful and achieve real change, one of the first things I say to everyone including the business owner is, **'You need to tell me everything, the good, the bad and the ugly.'**

If they tell me everything as honestly as they can, I can find out what's really going on very quickly. I can discover themes and develop strategies to resolve any issues, at a staff WIIFM (what's in it for me?) level, a management level and a business owner level.

By conducting these interviews one on one, I establish rapport with all staff because I'm not the business owner – I'm an outsider. Through this rapport and because staff can see I genuinely want to help them as well as the owner, they open up to me.

The information I learn can be quite astonishing. I have to say after nearly twenty years of working with staff and businesses, I'm rarely surprised by what I'm told and I haven't discovered anything too new. Why? Because business is business and most businesses, although varying in their areas of expertise, have similar problems revolving around their BPS. All that changes is the context.

The overarching theme among the staff is often frustration which can be caused by the little things like the tidiness of the kitchen through to the way the owner and other staff members treat each other, and the differences in how everyone is valued. This all comes out in the question and answer wash.

After I have completed all interviews, I then conduct a SWOT analysis (strength, weaknesses, opportunities and threats) to pull out the key themes and identify the real issues, new boundaries and expectations which need to be addressed. Following that, I help the business owner determine and reset the new priorities, focus and targets so everyone in the business can move forward, together.

These ideas and strategies are discussed with the business owner to ensure they resonate with what they want to do and where they believe the business is heading. The reason I discuss themes rather than 'this person said this and this person said that' is to ensure I maintain rapport, confidentiality and trust with all involved.

When delivering this information to the owner and staff in my half day Past Workshop, I highlight how the business is going to change bit by bit and explain everyone's key role (including the owner) within this process. Staff come on board because I have established trust and rapport in the interviews, and they can see how the information they confided to me has been translated into something tangible and relevant. It's also in this workshop that I'll address any attitudinal issues – for example cleaning, punctuality, roles and responsibilities etc. – in a balanced, serious but fun way.

I encourage my clients to hold this workshop on a Friday afternoon where it is followed by food and drink (or what I call 'The Wake') which I'll explain in more detail when I address the Attitude component of the PLAN.

Landscape

The second step in the PLAN is to look at the **landscape**. I've already talked about leadership which is certainly part of it, but what I'm focusing on here is the physical landscape:

- What does the office look like?
- What's the state of everyone's desk?
- What do the electronic files look like?
- What do the physical files look like? (Or is there no filing system at all?)
- How many emails are still sitting in inboxes (and sent mail) and do they need to be kept?
- How does the workplace landscape feel when people walk in the door?

The reason I ask these questions in the *Establish* the **PLAN** step is that a cluttered space often goes hand in hand with a cluttered mind. This results in feelings of being overwhelmed, frustrated and not knowing where to begin because the owner can't see the wood for the trees.

Remember: We can't all work and operate in the same way to get the best from ourselves.

There is absolute legitimacy and power in changing the behaviour of those people (which may also include you as the business owner) who move piles of work from the desk to the floor at the end of the day, and then back to the desk again the next morning. Not only are these people *not* being productive, but they're also jumping from job to job, client to client and task to task which means they're multitasking rather than maintaining single-minded focus. Multitasking is not an efficient way to work.

Remember: If you DARE to *Lead*, you're the role model for everyone in your team to follow.

I encourage you now to have a look around your office workspace. Have a look at what it looks like, whether it's the office at home or at your premises. As you look at the Landscape, it's important to examine your electronic and physical files. Do they make sense? Is everyone filing documents in the same folders? When were the files last decluttered properly or is that task still on the To-Do list?

One of the most common things I'm asked in presentations is to outline my filing structure. Setting up categories in a logical order that's easy to follow doesn't come naturally to most people so if this sounds like you, here's my rules of thumb:

- Use colours to categorise files such as green for clients (green = money)
- Follow the four D's
- Create a folder titled *Still to Look At* or *Park It* so you can declutter as you go (and feel like you're getting somewhere)

The idea behind the four D's is for every piece of paper, email or information that comes into the system to be actioned immediately, using one of these four D principles:

- Do it
- Diarise it
- Delegate it
- Delete it

You might be thinking this applies to you, that you need to do it but you don't have the time. Rather than giving in to the Time Wolf, I suggest you start decluttering in short sharp bursts of time e.g. fifteen minutes a day.

I prefer to declutter in one big go – ripping everything out of the office, going through it slowly and then moving everything to its new spot – but my personal life and running a business don't usually give me the luxury of large blocks of time. I'm sure it's the same for you so working in fifteen minute chunks of time is manageable. This is a great transition strategy which will enable you to chip away slowly and still complete your important (money train) work.

Imagine if you did this for fifteen minutes a day. It may not sound like a lot I know, but it all adds up. That's over an hour a week of sorting and decluttering which you weren't doing previously. This is a simple yet powerful tool to get you and your business back on track. The trick is to make sure you go back to your parked folder and action it. Otherwise you've just moved the mess from one folder to another.

Attitude

Although I'm sure we all think of **attitude** differently, a colleague of mine gave me the best definition: *attitude is the combination of your words (what you say) and actions (what you do)*. I now build on what I have said in the Past component and bring these ideas into my Past Workshop. This is where I challenge both owners and staff to reflect and identify key ideas:

- What is my attitude?
- What attitude am I bringing to work every day?
- What impact does my attitude have on my colleagues and clients?

These days many of us spend so much time at work (not to mention travel) which can add up to almost a quarter of each and every day. If we don't come to work ready and raring to go with a smile on our face, it can be much more difficult to get through the day and it can affect clients and everyone else around us. It's very easy to tell staff and ourselves that it's our personal life and we prefer to leave it at the door, but that's not always easy to do. It can be very hard to split ourselves into these two personas: one personal and another that's the business owner/employee. But we must remain conscious of it.

A key component of attitude is looking within yourself and noting what you see:

- Am I coming to work cranky every day? If so, am I calling myself on it?

- Do I have staff coming to work cranky every day? If so, am I calling them on it?

- Am I talking to staff to find out what's going on with them, what's bothering them and asking if there's anything I can do to help?

- Is there something my staff needs assistance with? Is there some underlying issue that hasn't been addressed in the past and has now come to the surface?

- If there is something I can do to help the situation that will, in turn, help my business?

- Have I thought about whether my staff are still the right fit for my business? If not, what can I do?

Do you want a business where everyone is happy to come to work and love what they do (including you)? As I've mentioned previously, leadership comes from the top. To achieve this, you have to look at the cause of any inappropriate attitude that is no longer acceptable within your business. Once you have identified any attitude issues, what action will you take to change or remove it?

As part of my Past Workshop, I also recognise that there is power in people venting the past. If you don't find out what's happened in the past and you don't see where people are at now, it makes it very difficult for anyone to truly move forward. If you don't do this, people will continue to carry the baggage of the past into the new change and not move forward at all.

Result: You're back to where you were before you invested time and money into changing the business.

In closing my Past Workshop, but before the wake is held to grieve the old organisation, bury the past and move on the next day, I ask everyone, including the business owner, to complete their 'baggage' form. This is their time to reflect quietly on what's been said and proposed during the workshop; and be honest about what baggage they are still carrying regarding the business, the owner, other team members, their role and how they work within the business.

As part of this process, everyone has to identify the things they need to leave behind so when they walk back in on Monday morning after Friday's workshop, everyone starts again with a clean slate. No baggage.

This very personal and powerful yet simple exercise often results in immediate change when coupled with three things:

1. Recognise and vent the past, then get rid of it.

2. Take the good into the future.

3. Look at what's been learned to see what needs to be left behind and what needs to be taken forward.

Without expressing these concepts, it can be difficult to move forward. And this isn't just true in business; it's also true for relationships outside business and work.

Numbers

Once you've vented the **past**, addressed the **landscape** and your **attitude**, it's time to look at your **numbers**. These include not only the numbers holistically for the business but the specifics including:

- How many clients do you need each year, each month and each week to meet your minimum financial targets? How many do you need to meet your stretch targets?

- How much does it cost to keep the doors open each week?

- What are your expenses each month?

- Which are your most expensive months?

- What's your break-even point? How does this work for different products and services?

- How much cash do you need each month?

- What is costing you money that is unnecessary?

If I'm now freaking you out because you don't know the answers to at least one of these questions, isn't it time you got serious about your business and figured this out? After you've answered the questions, if you don't know what the information means or how you can find out the financial position of your business then ask your accountant, bookkeeper or business colleague to teach you. Enrol in a one day workshop where you will learn to understand your business numbers or read a book on the topic. Whatever you do, you need to get on top of this *now*.

Although I took accounting at school and uni, I'm not an accountant and at times I don't know my own numbers as well as I should – something my Accountability Group and Masterminding Buddy keep reminding me: 'Yes but what are your numbers? What are your targets? How and where will you gain new clients?'

If you are the Reluctant Business Owner, this is probably not your strength either but don't fall into the trap of thinking the financial numbers don't matter because the accountant or bookkeeper looks after all that. Your financial numbers do matter, and no one should know them better than you. Otherwise, you might find yourself running an expensive hobby instead of the simple, profitable business you love.

Say you have a financial target for the year e.g. you want a turnover of $250K but you mightn't have a clue how to achieve this. Maybe you don't have the desire to keep on top of things and monitor the numbers every day to see if you're hitting your targets or the knowledge to make adjustments. Now I know you know it's up to you to do this. So if you're not on top of your numbers, why not?

Unfortunately, too many business owners get caught up in the hype of 'turnover' talk rather than 'cash flow' and 'profitability'. I've seen a few million dollar turnover businesses that don't have the cash they need to pay the bills, and they certainly aren't living the million dollar lifestyle. This is often because their decisions about their business and people need to change, and systems need to be streamlined or overhauled to increase productivity and profitability.

If you've fallen victim to the 'Turnover Trap', please remember the famous financial saying known as the Banker's Mantra: 'Turnover is Vanity, Profit is Sanity but Cash is King.' Another variation on this mantra is: 'Cash is Reality.' Regardless of which saying connects with you, hopefully you get my point and understand that starting today, your focus *must* be on your numbers.

Taking into account industry specific benchmarks, an easy way to remember how to view expenses is to think in terms of thirds. One-third covers wages/drawings, one-third is for expenses/overheads and the final third should be profit.

Obviously you can creep more into your profit if your wages or drawings and expenses and/or overheads are more than 66 percent (say 70 or 80 percent). But if they're more than 80 percent, you're diminishing your profit. I suggest you start looking at ways to reduce these expenses and streamline your processes to increase productivity which in turn increases profit.

Remember: You need to know your numbers in relation to expenses, and also the numbers you need to meet each week, month and year to reach your overall turnover and profit targets. Do you know how many clients you need for one or more of your services each month to achieve this target? What do you do if halfway through the month you're not even close to this magical number?

I know for many service-based businesses, this can often be a tricky calculation and maybe this is the same for your business. This is because they provide a number of services to clients, all at different price points, and the number of clients they need to meet their desired target depends on the service each client selects. Often it's hard to predict what type of training or package people will sign up for each month; for me it could be one of my retainer packages, a one day strategy session or my services as a keynote speaker.

My advice is to work out your numbers, service by service, on the assumption you will only have clients engaging you for that particular service so you can target the right marketing strategy to achieve this. Then, as the month goes on, you can work the numbers again, based on what has come in and then develop an alternative strategy to address any shortfalls. To achieve the best-case scenario each month, it's important to be on top of your numbers should the worst-case scenario raise its ugly head.

This process will also assist you to answer these questions once and for all:

- Are you running a hobby or a profitable business?

- Do you know your numbers and do you watch them every day?

- Do you need help with this to turn your business around and avoid becoming a Rundown Business or, worse still, a Closed Business?

Everyone needs a little help sometimes. If you want real change in your business, it's vital to engage your people in the process and support them as they vent the past.

Some of you may be reading this and thinking you do this already because you talk to your staff all the time. And that's great and yes, you should be doing that. But there's a lot of power in having someone external to your business talk to you and your staff to find out if there are other things afoot, and suggest ways for getting to the root cause of any problems. It's also an opportunity to gain access to those innovative ideas from staff members who maybe don't feel comfortable bringing their ideas to you directly.

I'm not saying this simply because I'm a Troubleshooter and that's what I do. I have proven, time and time again, that I can say exactly the same thing as the business owner has been saying to their staff members, but because it's coming from an outsider, it will be received differently. The behaviour of staff will almost certainly change and the issue will be resolved because the perceived value is greater when it comes from an outsider.

Frustrating I know, but I've seen it over and over. Every business needs help and outside advice, and every successful business has this philosophy built into their process. This is why is it essential and invaluable to be part of Accountability Groups, Boards and Mastermind Groups; and having a mentor, business coach, buddy or someone else who will give you impartial advice.

I am part of an Accountability Group which meets for breakfast every Saturday. It's fantastic because I can bounce ideas off them regarding possible marketing strategies, partnership opportunities, new products and services etc. and gain an idea of what they think. Although I can simplify processes and information for everyone else, I struggle to do it for myself because I'm too close to my own business. My Accountability Group simplifies my message to ensure it hits my target market in the best way possible.

This group of amazing people also gives me support when I need it and keeps me on track with my key priorities and focus for the week, month, quarter and year. It has changed my business and myself immensely, and all for the better. I wish I'd met them all years ago and I'm so very grateful for their ongoing help and support.

Have you got something like this for your business? Who is helping your business aside from you and your team? If you don't have something like this, why not? How quickly can you turn this situation around? Trust me, the time and money investment will be worth it.

THE POWER OF DELVING INTO THE PAST

One of my clients showed me a very innovative and powerful way to complete the baggage forms and truly embrace the messages of change from my Past Workshop. As it was a building designer business, the owner decided to build a small cardboard coffin. On Friday, when the workshop was over, everyone placed their folded baggage forms into the coffin and we went outside. The coffin was then burned in a bonfire, after which we went back inside for food and drinks. It was very symbolic and powerful imagery to finalise the change process. It was also a lot of fun.

What this business owner did the following Monday blew me away, although he didn't tell me about it until our next debrief a fortnight later.

On Monday morning, as his staff arrived for work, he greeted every one of them at the door with a handshake and a welcome to the business which took the staff by surprise. The power of this simple gesture not only reinforced his commitment to the changes he and his team had agreed to at Friday's workshop, but it also demonstrated he was serious about putting the old organisation to bed because change was going to start *today*.

Solution

His actions triggered, within each and every staff member, all the key messages from the workshop about new boundaries, expectations, acceptable and non-acceptable behaviour; and reminded them to leave the past behind for good and move forward.

He told me it had changed their **attitude** immediately. Talk about **DARE to Lead**. It was a very simple gesture, but with a very powerful outcome which is key to any change management process.

So how are you utilising the Power of the Past to help you build an even better business?

Building your business ..... one brick at a time

1. What are your top three Establish Wolves?

2. What is one thing you need to change about each Wolf to keep it at bay?

3. When will you start to make this change?

	My Establish Wolf is ...	What is 1 thing I need to change to keep these Wolves at bay?	I will start making this change ...
Example	*Numbers*	*Determine true financial position of the business*	*Tomorrow*
Establish Wolf 1			
Establish Wolf 2			
Establish Wolf 3			

Now you have *established your* PLAN, you can move on to the fourth step which is *Analysis* and this is when you start to **SMILE**.

Chapter 16

Analysis
When you start to SMILE

*You just have to pay attention to what people
need and what has not been done.*

Russell Simmons

The fourth step is about *Analysis* and the acronym **SMILE**:

- Systems
- Meetings
- Information
- Language
- Expectations

By now things are starting to run like a well oiled engine. Why?

You have put in place documented **systems** which everyone is using because they make sense and are easy to follow.

Meetings aren't happening just for the sake of it but are beneficial, productive and generally quite short. Imagine having a short meeting – is this wishful thinking or a reality?

The **information** exchanged within your business, between members of your team and your clients is valuable and meaningful because there's no waffle. There's clear purpose and understanding in the information which has been developed and communicated, both internally and externally.

The **language** in all facets of your business and with clients is positive and clear. Everyone is using consistent terminology across the business to describe your brand, products and services, in accordance with your key messaging.

And because of the documented systems, everyone is now clear on what is **expected** of them. A position description is not the <u>only</u> source of this information; it is just one part.

> If we don't take the time to see what's broken, how do we know what to fix?

People now actually know what to do within your business and because you've spent the time to document the necessary systems, the step-by-step procedures can be followed by anyone in the business as either part of a formal succession planning strategy or to help out when someone is on leave or has fallen ill.

If you undertake *Analysis* of what's actually happening in your business, compare this with what *should* be happening and then document the systems needed to address the discrepancy; your business will take off. It's up to you. Fix this and watch everything change for the better – and see yourself smiling more than once a day.

Building your business ..... one brick at a time

1. What are your top three Analysis Wolves?

2. What is one thing you need to change about each Wolf to keep it at bay?

3. When will you start to make this change?

	My Analysis Wolf is ...	What is 1 thing I need to change to keep these Wolves at bay?	I will start making this change ...
Example	Time	Review frequency of meetings	Tomorrow
Analysis Wolf 1			
Analysis Wolf 2			
Analysis Wolf 3			

The final step in building your BPS Roadmap deals with *Reality* and **CHANGE**.

Chapter 17

Reality is all about CHANGE

For changes to be of any true value, they've
got to be lasting and consistent.

Tony Robbins

T he final step in building your BPS Roadmap is *Reality* and this is all about **CHANGE**. You can have the best systems in the world, you can write great plans, you can have a clear vision and have everything looking good on the surface; but if none of these things translate into real change you can see every day, there's still more work to do.

You will know when your BPS Roadmap is *Reality* when you look at the acronym **CHANGE** and see each one of these signs present in your business:

- **C**onsistency
- **H**olidays
- **A**chievements
- **N**o (as an acceptable word)
- **G**enerosity
- **E**nergy

You hear **consistency** in the way you and your team speak to clients; you see it in your marketing materials and how your products and services are delivered.

You and your team have **holidays** and what I mean by holidays is no one – including you – feels the need to check into the office, either by phone or email because everyone knows the business is in safe hands. You, and any member of your team, can have a sick day and everything is still fine: the business doesn't come crashing down because there are simple back-up plans via the documented systems. And if you are the business, you have made a choice not to be available 24/7.

Achievements are happening: targets are exceeded, awards received, staff skills increased due to ongoing professional development or the willingness by everyone to do greater things.

The word **NO** is no longer a dirty word. It is your best friend because you're not saying yes to everything and everyone.

There's amazing **generosity** of spirit in your team because everyone wants to help each other. There's also generosity within the community as they help you build your M.A.D. and profitable business.

And the **energy** in the workplace is fantastic because everyone is happy to come to work and do their job.

When you have real **CHANGE** – once you're clear on your BPS – you will have the ultimate dream business. You and your team members come to work every day

> Real change
> takes time

knowing what to do and are happy to be there. Clients receive a consistent and quality experience. You're doing the work you love *and* you're able to take regular holidays, knowing the business is in safe hands.

But in order to have this *Reality*, there is one more thing you must understand: **real change takes time**. Please don't forget you always have to lead from the front and stay focused on maintaining your CLEAR BPS Roadmap. Once you do this, you can remove the shackles of the Reluctant Business Owner once and for all.

Building your business .....
one brick at a time

1. What are your top three Reality Wolves?

2. What is one thing you need to change about each Wolf to keep it at bay?

3. When will you start to make this change?

	My Reality Wolf is ...	What is 1 thing I need to change to keep these Wolves at bay?	I will start making this change ...
Example	*Holidays*	*Block out holidays for the year*	*Tomorrow*
Reality Wolf 1			
Reality Wolf 2			
Reality Wolf 3			

And that's all there is to it. You now have the tools and understanding to start building your BPS Roadmap for the simple, profitable business you love.

I could have finished the book here. However, as I'm all about solving problems, I want to provide you with not only the framework to take your business to the next level (my five step CLEAR process), but some simple practical solutions to move you from your current business house to at least the next one.

Let's now look at Part Three where I outline your foundation for success as you build an even better business, one brick at a time.

Part Three

Foundations for Success

Whatever you are, be a good one.

Abraham Lincoln

Chapter 18

Simplicity is the Key

When process is king, ideas will never be.

Steve Jobs

I'm sure you've heard of the KISS principle (Keep It Simple Silly) and the many variations on the acronym. Yet how many of you really practice this principle on a day-to-day basis?

In an age where people are bombarded with information via new mediums and new technology, at a pace that was unknown even five years ago, it's apparent to me that we all overcomplicate our lives and our businesses because we've lost sight of what is truly important.

Business owners can choose to simplify things, but too often they remain in reactive mode by band-aiding problems and ignoring opportunities rather than taking the time to take a break, step back and decide what is the best decision to make or option to undertake.

In my experience, simplicity is the one thing, above all others, which business owners crave which is why I'm often asked to make things easier and simpler for my clients. If this is what you really want, why not put in the energy to make it happen? There are many reasons why business owners are reluctant to embrace simplicity so here's three (with an extra one thrown in):

REASON #1: SIMPLE MEANS DUMBING IT DOWN OR CHEAP

There is an unfortunate stigma attached to the word *simple* which in turn creates resistance. Occasionally, I have clients who tell me they don't want a simplified business because it means they will have to 'dumb it down'. Simple means cheap, they say, and they don't want that: they want a sophisticated and professional business.

I completely disagree with this logic. I've had this conversation many times, even to the point of having to defend my position because I pride myself on being *The Simple Solutions Specialist*.

Simplifying anything – procedures, products, ideas or even a netball set play – is extremely difficult to do and a highly specialised skill. Try it yourself sometime. Review a twenty-seven step process and see how long it takes you to turn it into nine steps.

Luckily for me, making sense of things quickly and easily is one of my special skills, for which I am very grateful. (And by the way, it only took me two hours to turn twenty-seven steps into nine which saved my client three hours of administration time.)

REASON #2: I'LL SIMPLIFY AS I GO

You believe you can streamline and simplify things as you go, saving time. Unfortunately, you can't. When you start brainstorming, developing ideas and documenting procedures, you need to let the ideas flow to capture as much as you can while you're in the flow. The moment you start to analyse the steps or information in this stage, you lose traction and it will take so much longer to complete the task.

When I'm helping a client transfer how they undertake a process out of their head and onto paper, I quickly jot down the steps, in their words, using butcher paper and Post-it notes. Then I keep drilling down and asking questions like, 'How do you do that?' and 'What happens next?' I keep working the steps and working the steps until I have every minute detail documented.

Once that's done, we can go back over it all together and analyse each step to see what can be streamlined or eliminated because it's unnecessary or duplicated, thus making the steps as simple as possible.

REASON #3: I CAN DO IT ALL MYSELF

Unfortunately, you can't do it all yourself. Why not? Because you're too close to it: too close to your own work, processes and business. And this includes me. That's why, whenever I can, I ask someone else to review my work, marketing material, even this book. Ask someone else to look at your work with fresh eyes and provide a different perspective, because often, as I've said on a number of occasions, you see and read what you want to see – good or bad.

BONUS REASON: I NEED TO GET THIS APP

Normally, I stick to my rule of threes. But with so many technological distractions in the form of software and apps that claim to save you time and money and simplify your life, productivity and business, I believe it's worth mentioning this fourth reason.

I confess I'm not a techno-gadget guru but I have moved into this new world. I have an iPhone, iPad and Surface tablet, and I'm open to looking at new technology to see if it works for me and my clients. But what I actually see are many distracting shiny objects rather than tools to make our businesses and lives better.

Think about it: how many apps have you downloaded with the intention to use them every day, but instead have used them once for maybe a week, and then they sit idle, taking up valuable data space on your device? By all means, learn and try new things. But be aware that more and more people are spending their valuable time downloading apps to 'help' them, only to lose interest after the first week. Please ensure any tools or software you use or buy actually work for you.

Sometimes old school can be the best option, as confirmed by Ian Chappell, ex Australian cricketer. When asked which apps he uses, he said, 'Apps … all I need is a pencil, pad and eraser to work out my stats and notes.'

To end this chapter on simplicity, I will draw on one of the best examples and legends in this space – Steve Jobs of Apple who definitely lived and breathed the concept of simplicity. I read Ken Segall's book *Insanely Simple: The Obsession That Drives Apple's Success*. Segall was the advertising executive who worked closely with Steve Jobs for over twelve years, spanning NeXT and Apple. He started the i-frenzy by naming the iMac and helped develop Apple's famous 'Think Different' campaign.

To Steve Jobs, simplicity was a religion. It wasn't easy, but it was burned into his (and then Apple's) DNA which meant every idea was hit with the 'Simple Stick'.

Here are the eleven principles of simplicity Steve Jobs applied and embedded into everything he did which then became the culture of Apple:

> Simplicity is not easy but it can be contagious

1. Think Brutal: standards aren't for bending – not mean, just honest

2. Think Small: small groups of smart people

3. Think Minimal: sea of choices is no choice at all

4. Think Motion: never stand still – be wary of 'comfortable' timelines

5. Think Iconic: see the big picture, an image to galvanise an audience

6. Think Phrasal: never underestimate the power of a word

7. Think Casual: make a point quickly

8. Think Human: meaningful change in humanspeak – have a heart and metrics

9. Think Sceptic: take advice, not orders – expect the first reaction to be negative

10. Think War: it's good to have enemies – be prepared to battle complexity

11. Think Different: always original – never forget passion for your idea

All of these principles have key A-ha moments but I will share just one with you to illustrate the power of simplicity. Look at your meetings and see if you're inviting everyone to attend so they feel special, included and part of the team. Or do you invite only those people you need in the room for information, action and decisions?

In case you didn't realise it, meetings should primarily be about decisions and actions rather than information sharing. By taking this approach, not only will there be fewer people in your meetings, but by having a specific agenda and keeping to a timetable, your meetings will achieve the desired results.

WEEKLY TEAM MEETINGS CAN TAKE FIFTEEN MINUTES

One of my clients was frustrated with her Monday morning team meeting. It was taking half an hour to an hour and achieving very little except everyone stating the work they were doing for the week. She didn't want to devalue the team environment but felt the meeting was a waste of everyone's time. I suggested she change the meeting to fifteen minutes and focus on two sole purposes:

1. Outline the key priorities and targets for the week

2. Provide an opportunity for anyone to ask for the help or advice they need to complete their work

To support this change in strategy, we developed a shared document in Excel which each person, including my client, had to complete by 3pm Friday afternoon, ready for the Monday morning meeting. Everyone in the team had to outline key tasks for the following week. The owner reviewed these, developed her overall key business priorities for the week as well as any questions she had for staff which would be raised in the meeting.

It was each person's responsibility to update the document by the 3pm deadline. If they didn't, there was a consequence: the 'offender' had to pack and unpack the dishwasher for the week. If they continued to not complete this required task, this would be discussed at a performance meeting.

Solution

All staff had to read the document prior to coming to the Monday morning meeting so they knew what everyone else was working on to determine if help was required, either by them or for them.

The following changes were implemented for the team meeting:

- Limit of fifteen minutes
- Focus on key decisions and actions required rather than information sharing
- Create opportunities to ask for help in a supportive team environment
- Introduce accountability, responsibility and consequences.

Do you have this frustration in your business? Would this strategy or something similar work for you? Think of the productivity hours (wages) saved by cutting down a weekly meeting from one hour to fifteen minutes.

Steve Jobs said, 'Simple can be harder than complex. You have to work hard to get your thinking clean to make it simple. But it's worth it in the end because once you get there, you can move mountains.'

So remember Steve Jobs' philosophy: apply the Simple Stick to everything you do, in business and in life; and encourage big thinking but small in everything else. Resist the urge to apply corporate thinking and language to a small business.

Q Building your business ..... one brick at a time

1. Is Simplicity in your DNA, and if not, what needs to change?

2. What is the one thing (procedure, flyer, website page) you need to simplify so everyone understands it?

3. What are the three things you need to get done tomorrow to start simplifying your business?

I have used the number three extensively throughout this book and in the next chapter, I explain the method behind my madness.

Chapter 19

It's all about the Threes

Out of structure comes freedom.

Robyn Pearce

You will have seen the pattern throughout this book and know I'm all about the number three. I have repeatedly given three examples, three things to do, three pillars to building your BPS Roadmap; each of which are important and integral to success. Here is why I believe the number three is significant.

Today people have so many distractions at work and in their leisure time; and the internet with its infinite number of social media platforms, apps, videos and games adds to these distractions. With such an overload of information bombarding people 24/7 on various devices and via emails, it's no wonder many business owners and their staff are feeling overwhelmed and frustrated. They're doing a lot but getting nowhere.

Instead of taking the time to focus on key things that really matter, many people continue to multitask, believing they will eventually be successful. But that's not true.

I see so many people multitasking with multiple gadgets, often so disconnected from the people and life around them that they're not only missing the point about what's important, but by jumping from task to task with no focus or clear direction, they're wasting valuable time and energy.

Multitasking is no longer a skill you should admire or emulate. Productivity research now confirms multitasking achieves very little in the long run. Many people spend a huge amount of energy doing it, believing it impresses other people: *Look at them, they must be really busy and successful.*

New studies are showing that multitasking kills performance and may even damage the brain. Research conducted at Stanford University in 2014 found that multitasking is less productive than doing a single task at a time. Researchers also found people who are regularly bombarded by several streams of electronic information cannot pay attention, recall information or switch from one job to another as effectively as those who complete one task at a time.

And yet what do you see in the world today, particularly with the younger generation? People talking on devices and looking at screens as they walk down the street or through the shopping mall which causes them to run into people (like me) because they're focused on technology rather than being aware of what's happening around them.

Unfortunately, many business owners display the same behaviour so how present and engaged are you really … with yourself, your staff, your clients, your friends, your family? Are you that person who answers the phone at the movies, theatre, museum, sporting event and then whispers, 'I can't really talk now.' Well, if you can't really talk now, *turn off your phone.*

This also applies to those people who leave their phones on during meetings when they should be focused solely on their client. Instead, their phone rings, they answer it and tell whomever has called them, 'I can't really talk, I'm in a meeting.' Again, if you're in a meeting *turn off your phone.*

Just because you have a phone and are more accessible than ever before, it doesn't mean you should be available 24/7. I remember the days when I had to physically go back to the office to get my phone messages. Do you? If so, can you also remember how good that was, how much more work you completed and how refreshed you used to be because you were not on call 24/7?

If you don't know what this means or could use some help remembering, here are the baby steps you need to take (and you will thank me, just maybe not initially while you're going through withdrawal):

- Turn your phone to silent when you're in meetings, at an event or any other place you should be quiet and considerate of other people (including on public transport)

- Don't check your messages while you're in a meeting or at an event

- Don't return calls while you're in a meeting, at an event or any other place you should be quiet and considerate of other people (including on public transport)

I know turning your phone to silent can be a massive step to take, but I assure you, it will be okay. Once you've conquered this first small step and moved to the instinctive habit of turning off your phone when you're in meetings or at events, life will be so much better. There will be less glaring and muttering behind your back, and less tutting and turning of heads to see who's talking on their phone.

The only time your phone needs to be left on in these circumstances is if there's a family or medical situation, or you're expecting an urgent call that absolutely must be taken. If you're not sure what urgent really means, think back to the days when you had to wait until you returned to the office to receive your messages. This will clarify your definition of urgent.

You may be wondering what all this has to do with the number three. As one of my mentors, Keith Abraham, reminded me, 'Success is about having single-minded focus so you will not be distracted by shiny objects.'

I have always shown my clients and presentation audiences the power of three as well as using it in my own rituals and planning tools. There should only be three high level priorities for your annual financial target. Two examples of key priorities from my business have been the development of new products and services and the raising of my profile, of which publishing my two business books were key outcomes to achieving this.

With these three key priorities in mind, I then build my twelve month plan and outline the tasks I need to complete to achieve them. Then I break it down even further. If these are the three key priorities for the year, what are the three things I'm going to do this quarter (in the next ninety days) to help me achieve this outcome?

I map that out and then drill down further. What are the three things I need to do this month? What are the three things I need to do this week? What are the three things I need to do today to keep me on track and focused?

This simple but effective strategy enables me to work *on* my business rather than just *in* it.

What are your own three key strategic priorities for the year? Do you have a similar strategy which keeps you focused? If not, would this strategy or something similar work for you?

Can this be challenging? Absolutely. To achieve three key priorities for the year, you have to have a clear mindset and maintain your single-minded focus, even if that focus is for the 30 minutes

> Maintain your single-minded focus

you've allocated to complete a task to ensure you're not distracted by other shiny objects such as email.

Imagine what it would feel like to do just one thing for thirty minutes and do it really well because you have remained focused? If you're not distracted, you'll not only find yourself powering through the task with no errors, but you'll probably finish with time to spare. Wow, time to spare. For many business owners, that is an unheard of concept. Imagine what you could do with a spare five minutes? Stretch your legs, pat the dog, make a phone call or say hi to your family.

Otherwise, before you know it, it will be 31 December and you'll be reflecting on another year gone by and wishing you had done more, thinking about the things you never got to do and remembering all the things you have forgotten to do. Then you'll get into should-have, could-have and would-have thoughts which are counter-productive because what's done is done.

Building your business ..... one brick at a time

1. What are your three key priorities for this year?

2. What are the shiny objects you need to turn off or avoid? (For me it's Candy Crush on my phone.)

3. What are the three things you need to get done tomorrow to starting building your dream business?

Owner CEO Manager	My Key Priorities are ...	What is 1 thing I need to change to keep the shiny objects at bay?	Tomorrow I need to do ... to start building my dream business
Example	Re-develop the website	Turn off the phone for an hour	Review website layouts I like
Priority 1			
Priority 2			
Priority 3			

In these last two chapters, I have emphasised the significance of remaining focused to maximise your time. Now I'll take this idea one step further and show you the true Power of an Hour.

Chapter 20

The Power of an Hour

The way to get started is to quit talking and begin doing.

Walt Disney

When I ask business owners, 'If I had a magic wand and could fix one thing in your business, what would it be?' invariably the most common answer is, 'Can you please give me more time?' This chapter is all about providing you with tips to get back an hour a day.

But before I reveal these simple solutions, let me first share with you the power of an hour.

For many people, the thought of getting back an hour a day seems unattainable. But it really is easier to achieve than you think. And like the many examples and ideas I've shared with you already, it's about applying them consistently, each and every day, so strategies and techniques move from occasional tasks to ingrained habits you do automatically.

One of my business mentors, Keith Abraham, who is all about inspiring people to live passionately, believes developing daily and weekly rituals is one of the tools for success. In his blog 'You Can Change Anything in 63 Days', he writes:

> Why 63 days? Well, it takes 21 days to introduce a new habit – not to replace a habit, which is often talked about in personal growth books. I call this stage combative, as you are still battling with the habit you are trying to replace. The next 21 days is a stage I call cohesion, where the two habits co-exist: it is still a struggle but not a battle.
>
> The old habit is waiting for you to become vulnerable or your resolve to weaken so it can gain the upper hand. Then the final 21 days is a stage I call conquering, where your new habit takes over totally. You become very consistent with it, and it's now too uncomfortable to even do the old habit and feels like something is missing in your life if you don't do the new habit.
>
> Now the secret here is not to try to change too many things at once, as creating a new habit takes intention and attention. So just pick one new habit, ritual or routine you want to introduce into your life. Don't look for perfection, just turn up every day and do it. Now when I say turn up, I mean turn up! Often people set a new habit to exercise for 45 minutes daily, but the habit needs to be a little broader. The goal is to start to exercise daily. So it could be 5 minutes or 10 minutes or 20 minutes.
>
> Don't pursue excellence initially, pursue *consistency*.

With that in mind, what is an hour ... really? It is sixty minutes which could be chunked down into:

- 1 x 60 minutes
- 2 x 30 minutes
- 3 x 20 minutes
- 4 x 15 minutes
- 5 x 12 minutes
- 6 x 10 minutes

But first you have to do things smarter so the hour comes more easily, regardless of which chunking down combination you apply. And why is that important? Because time = money.

$$TIME = MONEY$$

Imagine if you could 'get back' an hour a day by doing things differently. What would that look like? What would that feel like?

Using an hourly charge-out rate of $100 (the value you place on your knowledge and skill), saving an hour means your earnings would look like this:

... per hour	$100
... per day	$800
... per week	$4000
... per month	$16,000
... per year	$192,000

Initially, you may not see this figure (savings) on your profit and loss statement or in your bank account, but if you worked smarter, not harder, you would eventually see this figure in your bank account. How? Because of the many ways you could use this extra hour:

- Develop a profitable partnership
- Submit a winning tender
- Gain new clients

- Develop new products and services
- Take a holiday so you don't suffer from mental overwhelm and have to take time off

This is the power of an hour and why it's so important to develop habits slowly, enabling you to become more proactive than reactive in managing your business. Remember in the Simplicity Chapter when I saved a client three hours by simplifying one process? That is the power of an hour – three times over.

And remember, it's not about finding one hour in a chunk, though if you can that's great; it's about finding one hour over the working day. So if you are struggling with focus, maybe consider adopting the Pomodoro Technique, originally created by Francesco Cirillo and used by people to increase their productivity and work more effectively.

Pomodoro Technique

The technique enables you to work in short sharp bursts during your day as well as taking regular breaks.

Short intervals

- 25 minutes on with 5 minutes off
- every 4 to 5 Pomodoros, you take an extended break

During each Pomodoro, you close down all distractions including phone and email so you can focus solely on the task at hand. Pomodoro tasks could be reviewing your numbers, writing an article/blog, developing a new product or service or completing a 'procrastination' task.

The 5 minute break is to gain time and space from both the task and your computer so get up, stretch, make a drink ... anything which keeps you relaxed but keeps the blood flowing. After this 5 minute break, you're ready to focus on another 25 minute burst.

Do you use the Pomodoro Technique already? If not, is this something you will build into your workday? Imagine what you could complete if you only did two Pomodoros a day. Imagine if you did four, six or more.

In addition to the Pomodoro Technique, here are my twenty-seven tips to get back an hour a day. You probably already do some of them occasionally, but now it's time to do these tips *every day*.

TWENTY-SEVEN TIPS TO GET BACK AN HOUR A DAY:
(in no particular order)

1. Turn off all bells and whistles on your email program.

2. Set up rules so emails move automatically into organised folders rather than into an overflowing inbox.

3. Develop weekly rituals and stick to them.

4. Turn your phone to silent (or even better, switch it off) for at least an hour a day of uninterrupted time.

5. Have an answering machine or service so you can be 'offline' for at least an hour a day. However, for this to work, you also have to turn down the volume. (It may seem obvious but when I suggested to a client they purchase an answering machine, they told me they had one but it didn't work. 'Is it broken?' I asked. 'No,' they replied, 'but what happens is the phone rings and I stop working so I can listen to the message to see if I need to call them straight back.' My look said it all.)

6. Eat That Frog! Brian Tracy developed this concept to overcome procrastination and ensure people focus on what's really important. If you're not familiar with this concept, watch the clip at bit.ly/PaDXVA and then just *do* it. (I have a page of cute frogs which I laminate and give clients and workshop participants, as well as use on my whiteboard. If you would like a copy, please go to my website and send me an email.)

7. Focus on doing your three things every day and then move onto the rest.

8. Work out your hourly rate (your value) and then ensure you're spending as much time as possible on activities that add value to your business (and equate to this high-value rate).

9. Spend time working out your numbers to ensure you cover how much it costs to keep the doors open (which includes paying yourself). There's no point in doing a job if, at the end of the day, you've only been paid twenty dollars per hour, regardless of the amount shown on the invoice.

10. Watch out for shiny objects – those things which distract you from your key focus areas. For many business owners, the biggest distraction is social media; the newest necessary evil in business. If this is you, look at tools like Hootsuite which can schedule your social media posts across multiple platforms.

11. Use a timer to limit (or focus) your time on particular activities and stop when it dings.

12. Look at alternatives to email when managing your tasks. Many businesses now use software like Asana and Slack to manage tasks and communication within projects and teams rather than clogging up emails.

13. Use Post-it notes – virtual or paper – to manage the lists upon lists that highlight what needs to be done, by whom and by when.

14. Have a day without your mobile phone. Or better yet, a Technology Free Day. Some businesses have also implemented an Email Free Day across their entire organisation to not only get people up out of their chairs and talking to each other, but to help them become more proactive rather than reacting to every email or phone call.

15. Spend an hour working somewhere other than your office. You'd be amazed at how much clarity and productivity come with a simple change of scenery, be it the beach, rainforest or coffee shop.

16. Don't be out of the office every day. Help educate yourself, your team and your clients to the times and days you take meetings so you're building a more proactive business. Of course, you need to be flexible to meet a client's requirement if it doesn't fit into this schedule, but it should work at least eighty percent of the time. This simple change will help you to start running your business your way rather than having everyone else dictating the terms.

17. Be the Tortoise and not the Hare. Don't always be in a rush to agree to everything. Instead, take a breath and see what saying yes actually means – for you and your business. Acting as the tortoise for even five minutes is better than always being the hare.

18. Do it. Diarise it. Delegate it. Delete it. The four Ds are a simple way to remember how to deal with a task such as emailing. And, as you can see, there is no 'ignore it' because this strategy is all about making a decision about what to do next, even if that's just to diarise to deal with it in an hour's time.

19. Spend the last thirty minutes of each day decluttering and planning for the next day.

20. Only check emails three times a day. To help educate your team and clients about how you work, add a note to your email signature like mine: *I only check emails three times a day so if it's urgent, please call me.*

21. Work out what times during the day you will return phone calls e.g. advise staff or have on your mobile message. *Unless I'm in meetings or presenting, I return phone calls between 11am and 12pm, and 2pm and 3pm each day.* This is a great way to educate your team and clients about how you work as well as determining what's important versus what's urgent.

22. Every quarter (four times a year), take at least one day out of your business, preferably in a different location and with an independent facilitator, to strategically review your numbers and key priorities against your annual business plan to determine any adjustments that need to be made, and then reset the focus for the next three months.

23. Develop your FAQs, place them on your website and give them to new clients.

24. Develop a **What Happens Now** document so clients understand all the stages throughout a project. This is particularly beneficial for businesses in the construction industry, and something I developed with a number of building designer businesses to reduce client questions throughout each stage of the build.

25. Spend fifteen minutes a day working on developing procedures for each position within the business.

26. Declutter your files, both electronic and physical.

27. Use a Bring-Up folder (1-31 expanding file) to store all reminders for that particular day. This can include details of meetings, client files and bills to pay.

These are all very simple techniques which will help you gain back some time in your day so which one will you start using?

Building your business ..... one brick at a time

1. What are your top three Time Wolves?

2. What is one thing you need to change about each Wolf to keep it at bay?

3. When will you start to make this change?

	My Time Wolf is ...	What is 1 thing I need to change to keep these Wolves at bay?	I will start making this change ...
Example	*Procrastination*	*Develop weekly rituals including morning and evening tasks I will do every day*	*Tomorrow*
Time Wolf 1			
Time Wolf 2			
Time Wolf 3			

Do you want to start building your dream business? Let me show you how.

Chapter 21

Build Your Dream

You can learn more from mistakes than you can from success.

Rod Macqueen

I f I had a dollar for every time a business owner or staff member has said to me, 'I wish things were simpler,' I would be a multi-millionaire. Unfortunately I'm not, but it amazes me how many businesses are overcomplicated by multi-page policies and procedures when simple flowcharts could be used, and client communications (letters, emails and the like) which are filled with unnecessarily complicated words and phrases.

Is it any wonder clients and staff are confused and interpret things incorrectly, are not sure of their roles and responsibilities, and may even choose to go and work for the competitor?

Many business owners are not spending the necessary time or effort to develop simple yet profitable businesses. So my question to you now, after everything you have read, is: Do you really want the simple and more profitable business? Because to truly achieve this, you have to invest time, money and effort; as well as be willing to make some changes, probably within yourself as well as in your business.

If you don't want to do this, stop reading now.

If you are ready, willing and able, here are the top seven factors for business success that will, once integrated, help you build a better business, one brick at a time.

Top seven factors for business success

1. **Work on your business as well as in it.** You have to keep developing your business to move it forward as well as undertaking the work that pays the bills.

2. Develop **business systems** by documenting all aspects of how you run your business. Use flowcharts, tasks and templates to capture this knowledge. Start chipping away at it today, using any downtime to get on top of this momentous task. Keep reviewing your systems to ensure they remain current and accurate.

3. Keep your **boundaries** with your clients and your team flexible, but it's important to remember they don't have to know everything or be involved in every decision. There needs to be balance.

4. **Business etiquette** is a lost art. You can email someone a message instantaneously but unfortunately, many business owners seem to have lost their business etiquette. This includes the common courtesy of thanking people for submitting resumes, proposals, articles and so on.

Remember: People have put in time and effort to provide you with that information or material. At least acknowledge it rather than ignoring it.

5. **Invest** extensive time and money on business development including networking and marketing when you're busy because you need to be ready for the uncertain downtimes.

6. **Learn to say no.** Remember the old days when there was no mobile phone or email and if you had an urgent message, you had to wait until you got back to the office? You don't need to be available 24/7. Is anything really that important?

7. You can have it all as long as you **accept the price**. When you make a choice to do things (or not), there is often a price; be it less time with family and friends, or less money or fun. You can't complain about the price you paid when you knew what that was at the time of making the decision.

> Build your dream business – one brick at a time

Building your business ..... one brick at a time

1. Are you following *The Procrastinator's Creed?* (Check it out on the next page – origin unknown.) If so, what's the one thing you need to change to keep this Wolf at bay?

2. How much time and money are you investing to build a simple profitable business?

3. When will you actually make this change?

The Procrastinator's Creed

1. I believe that if anything is worth doing, it would have been done already.

2. I shall never move quickly, except to avoid more work or find excuses.

3. I will never rush into a job without a lifetime of consideration.

4. I shall meet all of my deadlines directly in proportion to the amount of bodily injury I could expect from missing them.

5. I firmly believe that tomorrow holds the possibility for new technologies, astounding discoveries and a reprieve from my obligations.

6. I truly believe that all deadlines are unreasonable regardless of the amount of time given.

7. I shall never forget that the probability of a miracle, though infinitely small, is not exactly zero.

8. If at first I don't succeed, there is always next year.

9. I shall always decide not to decide, unless of course I decide to change my mind.

10. I shall always begin, start, initiate, take the first step and/or write the first word, when I get around to it.

11. I obey the law of inverse excuses which demands that the greater the task to be done, the more insignificant the work that must be done prior to beginning the greater task.

12. I know that the work cycle is not plan/start/finish, but is wait/plan/plan.

13. I will never put off tomorrow, what I can forget about forever.

14. I will become a member of the ancient Order of Two-Headed Turtles (The Procrastinator's Society) if they ever get it organised.

Chapter 22

Straw to Stick

You need to be surrounded by good advisers,
but you also need to trust your instincts.

Chris Hughes

aving been reminded of the signs of each of The Five Little Business Pigs as well as the five steps to get CLEAR on your Business, People and Systems (BPS) Roadmap, it's now time for you to start moving out of your current business house into something with more solid foundations.

The first and often the hardest thing you need to do is move from a very reactive house (or business that doesn't get blown away at the first sign of the Wolf) to a proactive business that is strong like the Brick house.

How do you do this?

You get help.

If you read any successful business owner's story, there will be a common theme and strategy which helped them achieve their success and it's this: successful business owners usually engage someone to act as a mentor or strategist for them and their business.

Who is helping you in your business? Who is able to help you look at things more clearly because they're not attached to it and in the trenches, living and breathing it every day?

If you don't have someone, I encourage you to think about it (and I'm not saying this because I'm a troubleshooting consultant). There is amazing value to having someone external to your business providing a different perspective because, as I continue to emphasise, most owners are too close to their own work, their team and their business.

In my business, I call on a few people who assist me in very different ways and have different areas of expertise to mine. When you invite someone external to your business to come in 'behind your wall', they will see things differently. Because you may not have this type of help yet, let me provide you with some simple strategies to move your business from Straw to Stick.

Embrace this question and decide your position, once and for all. Although this may not apply to you, you need to have alternative

> To change or not to change, that is the question

strategies in place when changes occur and be ready and willing to change; sometimes quite quickly. It's also important to remember that if you don't undertake regular maintenance on your business, you can find yourself back to a Straw or Stick business very quickly, and you don't want that to happen.

Moving to a Stick business is about defining what your business is about, gaining a great track record with your clients and understanding what has worked in the past (and what hasn't).

As I have outlined in the Business Pigs Chapters, there are three simple strategies for your BPS Roadmap to help move your Straw business to one made of Stick.

Straw to Stick

Business	People	Systems
Determine why you are in business and what you want to achieve	Be a leader by developing daily and weekly rituals that are easy to stick to and actually work	Develop an achievable annual business plan
Understand your numbers	Spend at least thirty minutes a day building your money train and marketing your business	Develop a cash flow spreadsheet to start tracking your numbers
Specifically outline the products and services for your specific/ niche market	Cultivate less attitude and more gratitude	Develop electronic and/or physical file structures and then declutter

SURVIVAL TIPS FOR A STRAW BUSINESS

Hopefully you're not a Straw business, but if you're not quite at Stick, there are three survival tips to help you on your way:

1. Just say no
2. Be willing to change
3. Adjust the attitude

Just say no

The first thing – and hopefully you can see a bit of a theme here – is learning to say no which can be hard when the money is coming in. I don't mean you should say no to every client who comes along. It's all about balance. It's about understanding the right clients to say yes to and those for whom you are unavailable.

I have lots of clients wanting me to help them, but until I develop online product options, realistically there is only one of me. To help me with this, I live by my diary and calendar; they are my best friends and help me manage my workload. I'm still not a fully electronic person – I'm a proud paper person which I realise does mean a bit of duplication – but this system works for me and that's one of my key messages: systems are not a one-size-fits-all approach.

My plan and diary is finalised by early January each year which means I've mapped out dates for client work, workshops, webinars, netball training and holidays (which include going to as many Hawks games as possible).

I also know when I have to be in the office to get particular jobs done which enables me to plan my business and my life. However, I've also allowed for spare time and capacity so my diary has the flexibility to meet both the needs of my clients (current and new) as well as changes to the market and economy.

When clients or your staff come to you with particular requests, are you able to say no because you *know* you don't have the capacity to undertake the task?

Conversely, if you go to your staff because you want them to do a long list of things and they already have eight on the go for that particular day, it's important to empower them to be able to tell you they can't do what you have asked. They should be able to ask you to specify what exactly you want them to do. This allows both of you to realise something in the priority order has to change.

Whether or not this is about how you manage your time, your staff manages their time or how you manage your clients, take the time to say no. You might still agree after ten minutes of deliberation, but that's still a better decision and a better outcome than agreeing immediately and realising the heartache of this decision. Maybe you will have to work weekends or miss out on a family gathering.

Be willing to change

This is about you, as a business owner and your willingness to change. Adjusting attitude is all about drawing a line in the sand and asking, 'Do I really want to stay in this Straw business I'm in, or do I want to move to either Stick or Brick?' You then have to recognise what is needed to take that first step.

Adjust the attitude

At this stage, if you're in a Straw business, you have to be willing to change your attitude as a business owner and that of your team. You have to be positive about working in this business. If you're complaining about your business, your clients and your team then maybe running a business is not what you should be doing with your life.

I've worked with registered training organisations (RTOs) for over twenty years, and unfortunately many working in the VET sector constantly complain about the Standards and the Regulator. My response to them is this: 'If you don't like compliance and you don't like change, don't work for an RTO or don't be one.'

Why am I this blunt? Because RTOs know the space they are playing in. Rightly or wrongly, it is highly regulated and changes frequently, but those are the rules. This means anyone working in an RTO should decide to play by the rules, find a partner or get out of the sector.

I'm wondering if my bluntness and tough love approach also applies to you and your business. If it does, changing your attitude would be the first step I encourage you to take to start building your new Stick business.

Building your business ..... one brick at a time

1. What are the top three things you need to do to move from your Straw business to a Stick business?

2. What's one thing you need to change to keep the Straw Wolf at bay?

3. When will you actually make this change?

	Top 3 actions to move from Straw to Stick	What is 1 thing I need to change to keep the Straw Wolf at bay?	I will start making this change ...
Example	Develop Annual Business Plan	Diarise 15 mins each day to chip away at this	Tomorrow
Action 1			
Action 2			
Action 3			

Chapter 23

Stick to Brick

When you find an idea that you just can't stop thinking about,
that's probably a good idea.

Josh James

I f you want to move from a Stick business to one made of Brick, it's all about slow and steady winning the race. You need to build your business one brick at a time, and you have to put in the time. If you're not willing to make the investment – an investment in dollars **plus** an investment in time to develop sustainable systems and processes, build strong foundations and put good systems in place – you will never move from a Stick business to a Brick business. You will continue to be thwarted by the Wolf which will continue to hover and if you're not careful, might actually come in.

It's always about work in progress so what's the one thing you can do every day to improve your business and make more money? How can you chunk down your processes? You will probably find that, at times, your business fluctuates between Stick, Brick and The Reno, depending on your clarity and single-minded focus.

If you really want to move your business to Brick, it's important to take the time to actually think about your next step. Your answers to these questions will help you determine your outcome.

> It won't happen overnight but it will happen

- How can I diversify my products and services?

- Am I going to change what I offer my clients?

- What other types of clients would benefit from my products and services?

- What new technology can I embrace to reach my clients virtually e.g. via Skype, Zoom, social media platforms and webinars; rather than meeting them face to face?

In this day and age of not a lot of dollars and not a lot of time, you can prioritise how you spend your time and money more selectively than even ten years ago. How can you open up more income streams that aren't dependent on you – your time, knowledge and expertise? So what's your journey, what's the pathway you're going to follow to make this happen?

Remember: You need to go beyond the great ideas and actually implement the *how* in order to make your dream business a reality. Otherwise, you risk going backwards.

When you're moving your business from Stick to Brick, here are three simple strategies to help you build your BPS Roadmap:

Stick to Brick

Business	People	Systems
Develop an organisational structure	Conduct 'Past' workshops to get you and your staff back on track	Start documenting procedures for each position within your business – aim for one a month starting with the Money Train (Sales)
Classify your clients	Review the workload and ensure deadlines are realistic and achievable; based on capacity, capability and a forty-hour week	Rotate staff into different positions to test procedures
Develop clear marketing messages	No emails or phone calls taken outside of office hours except on rare occasions. Work is completed within normal hours and what isn't done waits until the next day	Develop a style guide with specific colours and brand messaging – update marketing material including the website to ensure consistency

SURVIVAL TIPS FOR A STICK BUSINESS

Hopefully you're not really a Stick business, but if you're not quite at Brick, here are three survival tips that will help you on your way:

1. Know your numbers
2. Develop simple systems
3. Holidays are a necessity, not a luxury

Know your numbers

I've had too many clients (and workshop participants) who, when I first asked them if they were running a profitable business, told me an emphatic Yes. When I asked them how they knew, they invariably replied, 'I've got money in the bank so I'm all right.' Really? Just because you have money in the bank doesn't mean you're running a profitable business. You might have money in the bank today but when the bills come in tomorrow, all that money will be gone.

Understanding your financial numbers means looking at when your income streams come into play. Do you know when all your expenses come and in what month?

With my own business, I know my insurances – car, professional indemnity – come in sequential months. This means I have to plan for these big expense months and because these expenses are actually fixed, I also have to build CPI increases into my budget for each financial year.

Do you know what your expenses are going to be each month? It's all about cash flow and managing a budget. If you don't have a cash flow budget, then develop one very quickly.

Do you know when you need to find more clients so you gain more income in a particular month? Do you know your slow times and your hectic times? If you do – and that can be hard to manage sometimes – can you receive some of these payments earlier or move them to the next month?

Perhaps look at alternative arrangements for those June clients who want to spend their budgets by the end of the financial year because they have 'found' some money.

Taking payment in June but doing the work in July often happens in service-based businesses. Clients don't want to do anything for ages and then all of a sudden, they want everything yesterday and it's a big rush to get the work completed on time. If this happens in your business, is there a better way you can plan this with your client to avoid the last-minute dash? Have you been touching base with them throughout the year, providing value as well as offering your services so it hasn't just been sell, sell, sell?

If you're unable to receive full payment upfront for your services and you're not collecting deposits from your clients, you need to start doing this immediately. Collecting a deposit assists your cash flow, and is also a way to educate your clients about your processes and how you run your business.

Remember: If a client is not willing to pay your deposit because they can't find the money 'at the moment', you might find yourself chasing dollars from this client as the job progresses and that's something you don't want to be doing.

Now let's have a look at whether you're making money in your business, and I apologise if I'm teaching you how to suck eggs, but many business owners don't think about the dollars in this way.

You might have a business with one staff member earning $70,000 a year. That $70,000 is made up of salaries/drawings, but you also have to factor in ongoing business expenses because the staff member is utilising stationery and computers as well as being productive. And of course, you want to make profit from this person's work.

Here's a quick way to check your numbers to determine if you're actually making money or just covering costs (and I won't talk about the even worse situation).

> Salary/Drawings + all Business Expenses
> + **PROFIT** = Hourly Rate

You can break down a rate of $100 per hour into $60 (Salary/Drawings) + $30 (Expenses) + $10 (Profit).

It is important to clearly understand that $100, the hourly rate you charge, is actually made up of a number of components:

- $60 is roughly the hourly rate for a $70,000 salary figure
- assuming it costs you $40,000 a year to run your business, that equates to $20 per hour, the second component of the equation
- a profit of $20 per hour

But what if your rate is $80 or $90 per hour? Sound a bit scary? You have no profit at $80 per hour but at least you're not running at a loss.

If you charged this staff member out at $70 per hour, it's clear you would be making no money at all. You're covering their salary but you're not covering the actual running costs of the business – as they are associated with this staff member.

If you're not sure how to work this out, I suggest having a chat with your accountant or bookkeeper to find out the salaries you're paying yourself and your staff, and what your actual charge-out rate should be by incorporating *both* your business expenses at a percentage rate and your profit.

Now let's assume the $100 per hour gives you some profit. There's another step to this equation and this is the part many business owners often don't do well (or at all). You now have to determine, knowing the costs associated to keep your doors open, whether you're actually going to make money on an ongoing basis, on every job. Put another way, are you running a profitable business or just putting money in the piggybank?

Let's assume a client comes to you and says, 'I want you to deliver XYZ for my business.' You then sit down to work out the total cost to charge the client i.e. a value proposition not identified by an hourly or daily rate. To develop this fee, there are some costs (direct and indirect) to consider:

- Development/research time
- Time onsite to provide the service
- Travel (time and actual costs)
- Printing, if applicable
- Support/ongoing liaison

There may be many other things to consider, depending on the type of work you undertake. Based on these considerations, you then advise the client that in order to complete the work to their specifications, it's going to cost them $1500. This figure is based on the fact you believe it will take you or staff twenty hours to achieve all the desired outcomes.

You then have to find out from your staff member, preferably along the way but at least at the end of the job, how long it *actually* took to complete the work. If you don't ask this key question, how can you know whether you made money on this job?

Let me illustrate this point with a few examples:

- If it took twenty hours to complete the work, all is okay. You made a profit because the work was completed in the allocated timeframe.

- If the work was completed in fifteen hours, you're in an even more profitable position. More profit = happy days, and maybe there's a movie ticket to say thanks to the staff member for a job well done.

- If the work took twenty-five hours to complete, there's a problem. You have made no profit and, depending on your overall costs, you may actually have sustained a loss.

I realise this is probably the boring part for many business owners but it's one of the most important activities to undertake. Which business owner will you be from now on? One who neglects the boring bits (which is why they're running a hobby and not a business) aka The Reluctant Business Owner, or the business owner who understands and knows their numbers inside out?

There is another reason why it's important for you to gather the data on how long work takes to complete. If you don't track this information consistently, you won't be able to provide profitable proposals to clients rather than just guesswork. Without this information, how do you know if you're actually chewing into your profit?

If you only take one thing from my book, I hope it's about looking at your financial numbers to make sure you're really making money: I'm sure you don't really want to be running an expensive hobby business.

Develop simple systems

Whether you like it or not, documenting the knowledge in your head about how you run your business is essential to business success. Do you have policies and procedures in place for every position within your business so you have succession planning in place (as well as a saleable and scalable business)? If you're not sure how to go about this, your accounts person would be a good place to start (and that person could well be you: in my business, it's me).

Start documenting how you enter your payments and receipts into your accounts. What reports do you look at each year, quarter, month, fortnight and week? How do you enter your receipts into your accounting program; be it XERO, MYOB or a spreadsheet? If everything about your accounts remains in your head and your helpers don't know who to invoice because the desk or in tray is a mess, how can they help you make money?

Once your business becomes financially viable, one of the first areas to be outsourced is usually the bookkeeper position. Many small business owners often enlist the help of their wife, husband, partner or other family member to do this job, particularly in the early stages of the business.

Documenting these systems will save your sanity and will definitely make holidays more enjoyable.

Holidays are a necessity not a luxury

Many of you are probably laughing as you read this, thinking holiday, what holiday? I realise it may seem just a pipedream to have a three week holiday in some tropical resort because currently your cashflow (and workload) tells you this is not possible. By holiday I mean time away from the business, whether that's a day, a weekend or a few weeks.

I often travel to Melbourne for business and to see my beloved Hawks play at the 'G', and I always carry my notebook and pen with me. This is a simple but important technique because I never know when inspiration will strike. I'm always amazed by the number of times I'm watching a game and yelling support for my team when out of the blue, the gem of an idea for my business appears.

Why does this happen? Simple: I'm not in the office. I've changed my landscape to spark creativity, productivity and solve problems. And it doesn't just happen at Hawks games; it also happens on planes, in coffee shops, in fact anywhere. Just getting out of the office and sitting in the park to work on something can be a great way of tapping into your creativity. Give it a go and see what happens. I believe you'll find time and space to be very cathartic.

Writing this book created a huge challenge for me because I couldn't always escape the house, but I needed to write something every day or every few days in order to meet my deadlines. I knew the words wouldn't come sitting at my desk in the office especially as it gets very hot in the afternoon and the afternoon is my most creative thinking time. So I created a pop-up writing space and environment outside with things which would spark my energy and creativity. I could see my focus for that day and inspirational quotes on my flipchart. I covered the table with brightly coloured cloths and turned on my favourite music because I cannot write in silence.

It was brilliant. It proved so successful that I now set up my writing space as often as I can to create brochures, content for my workshops and webinars, as well as write articles and social media posts. I pack it down at the end of each session so it doesn't intrude on the rest of the house. It's such a simple thing, but it's amazing what power our brain provides us with when we allow ourselves to switch off and change our surroundings.

Where can you go to gain some inspiration and work *on your business* rather than *in it*? If you can't leave the office, can you create your own temporary space in another room to shift your thinking, be it to solve a problem, think of a new idea or just to refocus and gain clarity about what to do next?

Time out and a change of space are often undervalued. Do it more often.

Building your business ..... one brick at a time

1. What are the top three things you need to do to move from your Stick business to a Brick business?

2. What is one thing you need to change to keep the Stick Wolf at bay?

3. When will you actually make this change?

	Top 3 actions to move from Stick to Brick	What is 1 thing I need to change to keep the Stick Wolf at bay?	I will start making this change ...
Example	*Know your Numbers*	*Diarise 15 minutes each day to chip away at this*	*Tomorrow*
Action 1			
Action 2			
Action 3			

Chapter 24

Brick to Reno

If you can't feed a team with two pizzas, it's too large.

Jeff Bezos

A Brick business is all about managing your performance and that of your team, ensuring consistency of procedures and client experiences, and identifying further opportunities as a result of an improved marketing strategy.

Here are three simple strategies for your BPS Roadmap to help move your Brick business to The Reno.

Brick to The Reno

Business	People	Systems
Brainstorm all possible partnership opportunities for your current and new products and services	Create a culture of continuous improvement by encouraging and engaging staff to put forward new ideas and opportunities	Review and simplify all business systems including procedures
Determine numbers for growth to determine financial viability	Every person takes a proper holiday each year (minimum of two weeks at a time, preferably three) Week 1: holiday starts Week 2: start to unwind Week 3: slowly getting ready to come back to work	Develop procedures for new products, services and any new positions as you go
Regularly ask your clients for feedback on service delivery and ways to improve Conduct random mystery shopper or undercover boss activities to ensure clients receive a consistent and quality experience every time	Invest in two positions: CEO/operations manager to run the day-to-day operations; and a Business Development Manager to foster and create new partnerships	Develop partnership agreement templates and procedures

SURVIVAL TIPS FOR A BRICK BUSINESS

Hopefully you're on your way to The Reno business. But if you need some pointers, here's three key survival tips to help you on your way:

1. Manage performance
2. Marketing strategy
3. Regular maintenance

Manage performance

At this stage, the challenge I often see business owners grappling with is how to manage the performance of their staff. You have a great team around you and if you're like many of the business owners I see, you're probably too nice to them. You're probably not addressing the little things like punctuality, dishes in the kitchen, what it actually means to work in your workplace, following all the procedures etc.

Your staff members are probably not causing problems, but how can you be sure you're consistently managing the performance of each person? Are you letting the little things go? Are you watching your staff take client meetings? Are you randomly reviewing client work to ensure the standard is consistently high?

Just because your people are very pleasant to you doesn't mean they're not inadvertently hurting your brand in the marketplace and with clients. Often clients just walk, never to return again, because they don't always provide feedback about a *not so pleasant* experience; although these days, with so many people active on Facebook and Twitter, it's possible any negative feedback could be more public than you would like.

So it's critical to keep on top of your client service and ensure the quality standards of your products and services remains at a consistent level.

In a Brick business, it's all about managing and maintaining performance so my suggestion is, regardless of what time of year you employ your staff, place everyone on an annual performance review in June or December (whichever is the end of your financial year). This means you undertake formal performance reviews only once a year, and undertake some informal reviews along the way. This also allows you to set the outcomes for each team member for the upcoming financial year as well as your professional development plan for the next twelve months.

WHAT'S YOUR LIMIT?

Here is a key question to ask yourself: Have you set salary scales for all positions in your business? I had a client who continually gave his staff members pay rises each year which the staff obviously thought was fantastic. However, it created this expectation in the team: as long as everyone did a good job, every single person in the business would get an annual pay rise.

But what did this annual pay rise mean for the business? By not setting a ceiling salary by position (e.g. what the administration manager earned at the top level and how many steps it took to get there) the client had created an unrealistic expectation within the team. If the business didn't do well in a particular year and the client couldn't afford pay rises for everyone, there was a problem.

Solution

If you don't set an upper level for each position within your business, you may find you're paying $100,000 for an administration person because you have allowed their salary to keep going up and up every year. It's important to set increments and benchmarks as part of your human resources process, and often you will find there are four levels within each positional salary scale. As each person reaches the top level for their position, you can then look at other ways to reward your team (e.g. Gold Class tickets).

Remember: As I said in the M.A.D. Chapter, not everyone wants money as the reward for performing well in their role.

Marketing strategy

Often a Brick business has gained the majority of its clients by word of mouth. This means they have enough work or maybe even too much work which is a great problem to have. But for a Brick business to become The Reno business – either with more staff, different products and services or even by branching out into different industry sectors – this is the time to invest heavily in a marketing specialist to take the business to the next level. I would suggest initially outsourcing this function to a reputable, specialist organisation.

This investment could be for the following marketing strategies:

- Search engine optimisation (SEO) for the website so it appears on the first page of a Google search

- Create an inbound marketing campaign to attract your target market to your website and services, generating quality leads and converting those leads into sales

- Create a character to appear in a whiteboard animation video which could then be pushed out across social media channels

Whatever it is, the brand and messaging must remain consistent with the ultimate vision and purpose of the business, even down to the colours and fonts utilised. If the marketing messages aren't congruent with the business and its owner, the investment will actually do more harm than good.

Regular maintenance

What's the one thing you could do to make your business better and stronger? What could you consolidate to ensure there are no gaps in the bricks? What's your backup plan if you or your team get sick? How do people get paid? Who has keys to open the store or office?

To take your Brick business to the next level, it's all about the one percent change every day. You also need to be carrying out regular maintenance by looking at systems, processes and better ways to improve your business. No one wants to have a business which turns into the rundown house that needs to be shut down or demolished simply because it hasn't been looked after properly and treated with TLC.

The most important thing to remember with regular maintenance or, as it is more commonly called, continuous improvement, is the jigsaw puzzle is never complete. There

> A regular maintenance schedule ensures you do not become complacent and vulnerable to the Wolf

are always ways of improving a business. What impression about your business are you presenting to your clients? Is your website fresh and up to date or does it need some TLC? You should always be looking at different ways to improve your productivity and profitability. It's actually a good thing the puzzle is never complete.

A regular maintenance schedule ensures you do not become complacent and vulnerable to the Wolf

Building your business ..... one brick at a time

1. What are the top three things you need to do to grow your Brick business into The Reno business?

2. What is one thing you need to change to keep the Brick Wolf at bay?

3. When will you actually make this change?

Owner CEO Manager	Top 3 actions to move from Brick to Reno	What is 1 thing I need to change to keep the Brick Wolf at bay?	I will start making this change ...
Example	Develop potential clients mindmap	Diarise 15 mins each day to chip away at this	Tomorrow
Action 1			
Action 2			
Action 3			

The final chapter in this part of the book is all about strategies to bring life back into your Rundown business. Although you may think this isn't you and you want to take the easy option and skip this chapter, I encourage you to read it. It's a gentle reminder of what can occur when a business owner loses sight of what's important and stops building their time and money into their BPS Roadmap.

Chapter 25

Rundown to Resurgence

If you're not a risk taker, you should
get the hell out of business.

Ray Kroc

Y ou *can* skip this chapter if you're not in The Rundown business. Or you can make the better choice and read it, either to get the kick up the backside you need to get you and your business back on track or as a reminder of how quickly it can all change.

If you are in The Rundown business, there are some simple strategies you can undertake to start rebuilding your BPS Roadmap and turn your business back into at least a Straw business.

> Shape up or
> ship out

Business

Decide if you still want to be in business? If yes, determine what your business is made of:

- ☐ Straw

- ☐ Stick

- ☐ Brick

Now decide what needs to be changed in your Business, People and Systems (including you).

If you have decided NOT to continue in your business, what steps do you need to take to:

- ☐ Exit from the business

- ☐ Sell the business

- ☐ Close the business

- ☐ Get a job

- ☐ Retire

- ☐ Take a break

People

What do you need to change about your attitude and outlook on life so you can start to enjoy your Business, People and Systems (BPS)?

Are there any People on your team who could be better managed or even moved out of your business? This may be internal staff as well as external contacts, be it suppliers, friends and colleagues.

Systems

Here are three simple steps to build your Systems foundations:

1. Declutter your desk, office, physical and electronic files so you can start again with a clean slate.

2. Rewrite your Annual Business Plan.

3. Create new daily and weekly rituals which you will commit to and action every day, every week.

I have found two posts on Facebook which succinctly summarise my key messages for this chapter (written by Julie Tasker of Specialist PMC).

Although they both refer primarily to the New Year, the messages are also applicable to new beginnings, whenever you choose for them to start.

WHAT'S ON YOUR 'DON'T DO' LIST?

For many of us, the first day back at work in January is the start of our new working year. Some of us are the glass half empty type: *I have to wait twelve months for my next lot of annual leave.* Some are the glass half full: *What projects can I complete this year?*

But those of us who are true business entrepreneurs look at our business from all sides; the things we can do, the things we didn't do so well with last year; but we also look at what we DON'T want to do and why.

DON'T isn't a bad word in business.

We need to listen carefully to this word. Our business sixth sense often tells us when to put the brakes on. I can hear you say 'brakes on' in January. I must be crazy.

While many things you will read this month will be motivating you to jump in with new projects, no one will tell you to walk. Yes, WALK, not with caution, but with a clear direction.

Look and listen to your sixth sense this January and you may find that each new project you tackle this year has purpose for the long term benefit of you, your staff and your business success.

First mission of the New Year – learn when, where, why and how to use the word DON'T.

5 THINGS TO PURGE FROM YOUR BUSINESS

I often find it difficult knowing what I want to change in my business but have no problem knowing exactly what I don't want. So that's where I will start this year.

Excuses

It is simple to make a list of goals you want to accomplish in the new year, but it is infinitely easier to find reasons why you will not achieve them. Lack of time, money or energy for new endeavours is nothing new to anyone. The most successful entrepreneurs have the same problems, but the difference between them and everyone else is that they look beyond excuses and find resources to fulfil their dreams.

Shortcuts

Cutting corners and taking shortcuts can help you get things done, but too often one shortcut leads to another, and the next thing you know you are deep into a pattern that ultimately requires more time to fix. Taking shortcuts professionally will lead to embarrassing performance. Taking shortcuts personally will lead to strained relationships and compromised health. Eliminate the inclination to take shortcuts and understand that focus, hard work and dedication are the only things that lead to success.

Frustration

All business owners have plenty of distractions about which to get stressed. Unfortunately, stress and frustration only make these situations worse. It all puts strain on your colleagues, your personal relationships and most important, your health. It will drain you of the energy you need to focus on your goals. Find outlets for your stress and focus your energy on staying positive.

Blame

Good business owners are by nature at the top of the totem pole. Any failing in the business, regardless of circumstance, is ultimately their responsibility. Period. Sometimes this is a hard pill to swallow. Resolve to take responsibility for your actions and those of your business. Doing so will help you instead turn your attention to what is really needed: finding solutions and not focussing on whom to blame.

Clutter

I am a fairly organised gal. At the end of the day, I like my desk and email inbox clean. Unfortunately, I still have hoarding habits, keeping everything from receipts to files to emails for years on end. At the beginning of this year I decided to eliminate or archive anything that I have not read, worn or used since 2013. This includes everything from email to clothes to files (anything I was required to keep was scanned and stored in the cloud). The purge was amazingly refreshing, and it not only cleared out my closet and computer, it cleared out my anxiety.

If you can relate to any of these necessary purges, then kudos for recognising that you, like me, are guilty of them. That is half the battle to setting a better course for a new year or new beginning. Once you understand the habits that are holding you back, you can make meaningful resolutions that bring you closer to achieving your goals this year.

Building your business ..... one brick at a time

1. What are the top three things you need to do to turn your Rundown business into a Resurgent business?

2. What is one thing you need to change to keep the Rundown Wolf at bay?

3. When will you actually make this change?

	Top 3 actions to move from Rundown to Resurgence	What is 1 thing I need to change to keep the Rundown Wolf at bay?	I will start making this change ...
Example	Decide what the next step is to be	Be more aware when you hear yourself or see yourself demonstrating 'Rundown' business behaviours, and address it there and then	Tomorrow
Action 1			
Action 2			
Action 3			

Remember: If you remain the Reluctant Business Owner, you will never build the simple profitable business you love.

The CHOICE is yours.

If you decide to remain the business owner and turn your Rundown business into a Resurgent business, then I recommend you take these three steps:

1. **Decide** which business house you want to build.

2. **Commit** to what you need to do to get you and your business there.

3. **Action** what you need to do and this time, make it happen.

Get the HELP you need to support you and your business through this transition.

Part Four

If it's to be,
it's up to ME

If you really want to do something, you'll find a way.

If you don't, you'll find an excuse.

Jim Rohn

Chapter 26

What's Next?

Virtute non Verbis
[Action not Words]

St Rita's School Motto

The title of this chapter and the quote are intimately connected with me for two very different reasons. The quote was my high school motto. It's a philosophy I embraced at school and I do my best to live up to it every single day. The chapter title comes from one of my beloved TV shows, *The West Wing*. If you're not familiar with the show, President Bartlet's favourite phrase to his staff is: 'What's next?' This is their signal that he's ready to move on and wants to know the next thing he should be focusing on.

Here is my challenge for you:

- What's next for you and your business?

- What's the first thing you will do, once you've finished my book, which contributes to starting to build (or rebuild) your business, one brick at a time?

Or, instead of embracing *Virtute non Verbis* once you've finished my book, will you simply acknowledge all the simple strategies and great ideas you know you *should* implement, but do nothing? Will everything stay business as usual because, just like all your notes from every training program, book, webinar, chat with colleagues; the actions I recommend in this book will wait until you have more time, more money, more ... (insert excuse here)?

You may think that's too blunt and harsh. But that's my tough love approach which, when needed, appears by the truckload and I do not apologise for that.

So my question to you now is, 'Are you doing all of these simple strategies I've outlined in this book *every single day*?'

If you are, you must be in a strong Brick business that is renovating as I write this, so congratulations.

If you're not, what's your next step toward building a better business than you have today, one that is simple, profitable and one you actually love?

A business that doesn't keep you awake at night.

A business you enjoy going to every day (or as many days as you like).

A business giving you the freedom to work where you want and when you want.

A business that does more than just pay the bills and keep you afloat.

A business that isn't in Struggle Town.

A business you truly love and that gives you everything you ever wanted and more.

Wasn't that your dream when you first took the plunge into this world of business?

If you want to implement real change within your business, please remember:

- Build strong **foundations**
- Be the **Tortoise** not the Hare
- Have a weekly **ritual**
- Put business **etiquette** back into your business
- Realise **NO** can be your best friend
- **Accept** the price
- Have **another** set of eyes
- **Deal** with it – don't avoid it
- Realise it's all about **them** and not about you (*them* being your clients, staff, stakeholders, alliances, partnerships)
- Make profit and **cash**, not just turnover on the profit and loss statement

---

Q **Building your business .....**
one brick at a time

Where does your focus need to be right now, today?

1. **Business (Starting your business)**

2. **People (Managing your business)**

3. **Systems (Building your business)**

Remember: **FEAR** has two meanings and the choice is yours:

Forget Everything And Run
OR
Face Everything And Rise

The Choice is Yours – so what's your Choice?

The lyrics of this John Farnham song seem appropriate as a gentle reminder and nice summary of the messages contained within this book.

New Day

A new day coming, a change at last
All our problems, fade away in the past
New hope, new way
We start today
There's a new day coming, our way
Stormy weather, when things get rough
Empty promise, we've had enough
Looking down, the road I see
It's the future, the way it's gonna be
We're on our way again
We're back on our feet again
This time I know

J Farnham, P Buckle and R Fraser

Resources

I'm sure many of you have read or listened to many business books to help you on your business journey, so these titles may already be in your bookcase – or in your *Job Done List*, as stand-up comedian Jimeoin would say. But just in case, here are some of my favourites which include some business autobiographies as that's my usual reading genre.

Business

Any book by Australia's number-one bestselling small business author Andrew Griffiths
Blue Ocean Strategy - Renee Mauborgne and W. Chan Kim
Built to Last - James Collins and Jerry Porras
The E-Myth Revisited - Michael E Gerber
Finding Your Element - Ken Robinson
The 4-Hour Work Week - Tim Ferriss
Good to Great - Jim Collins
Insanely Simple - Ken Segall
It Starts With Passion - Keith Abraham
Key Person of Influence - Daniel Priestley
Networking Magic - Robyn Henderson
The Obstacle is the Way - Ryan Halliday
One Step Ahead - Rod Macqueen
Peaks and Valleys - Stephen Johnson
Rich Dad Poor Dad - Richard Kiyosaki

Six Thinking Hats - Edward de Bono
The Six Value Medals - Edward de Bono
Think and Grow Rich - Napoleon Hill
Value-Based Fees - Alan Weiss
Who Moved My Cheese? - Stephen Johnson
Hannah's Christmas Gift - Bruce Sullivan
Creating Loyal Profitable Customers - Keith Abraham
Getting a Grip on Time - Robyn Pearce
The Business Bakery - Julia Bickerstaff

Most autobiographies by business, sporting and iconic people including
Robert Kiyosaki, Nelson Mandela and John F Kennedy Jnr.

People

Awesome Authenticity - Jennie Gorman
Your Brain at Work - David Rock
Emotional Intelligence - Daniel Goleman
The E-Myth Manager - Michael Gerber
Fish and Fish Sticks - Stephen Lundin
Gen Y - Peter Sheahan
How to Feel F.R.E.S.H. at Work Every Day - Karen Schmidt
Keep 'Em Keen - Karen Schmidt
Leading Change - John Kotter
Making Fun Work - Kevin Ryan and Dennis Moore
The ME Myth - Andrew Griffiths
The One Minute Manager - Kenneth Blanchard and Spencer Johnson
One Step Ahead - Rod Macqueen
QBQ - John G Miller
UGRs - Steve Simpson
When the Rubber Hits the Road - Dr Brenda Jamnik
The Whole Brain Business Book - Ned Hermann
XYZ - Michael Grose
Your Employer Brand - Brett Michington

Systems

The E-Myth - Michael Gerber
The Mind Map Book - Tony and Barry Buzan
The Productivity Ninja - Graham Allcott
Get Stuff Done - Sam Harrop
The Tao of Twitter - Mark Schaefer
Social Media Secret Sauce - Adam Houlahan
Digitally Enhanced - James Crook

About Tamara Simon aka The BSi

It's not that I'm so smart;
it's just that I stay with problems longer.

Albert Einstein

Tamara Simon is the Simple Solutions Specialist known as The BSi, and she is all about solving small business problems with simple solutions. As a Speaker, Author and Troubleshooter, Tamara specialises in helping Reluctant Business Owners and Registered Training Organisations (RTOs) get CLEAR on their Business, People and Systems (BPS) so they build a simple profitable business they love.

With over twenty years' experience in business management, business improvement, organisational development and vocational education and training (VET), she has worked in over twelve industry sectors across public, private and not-for-profit organisations. She quickly cuts to the chase to sort out what's costing a business time and money.

Tamara's leadership and management expertise was recognised when she was a finalist in the Queensland Telstra Business Women's Awards and the Australian Institute of Management's Excellence Awards.

An accomplished speaker and trainer, Tamara has spoken at international and national business and VET conferences, and was voted by delegates as one of the top five presenters at Velg Training's National VET Conference.

Tamara was a Founding Contributor of fortnightly blogs for *Smallville*, the website for small business owners who think big.

Her articles have also been published in membership association magazines including *Women's Network Australia, Building Designers Association of Queensland, Master Builders Queensland* and *Velg Training*.

The Five Little Business Pigs is her first business book. Her second book – *The Five Little RTO Pigs: Helping Registered Training Organisations build simple profitable and compliant businesses* – is an adaptation of this one and is the first business book written specifically for RTOs.

In her spare time, Tamara loves reading autobiographies and crime novels; watching most sports, especially AFL and netball; coaching junior netball; and seeing stand-up comedians. She is also an avid member of the Hawthorn AFL Club, and both the Queensland Firebirds and Melbourne Vixens netball teams.

So why 'The BSi'? Tamara loves solving problems and watching crime shows so she is often called 'the CSI for small businesses'. Just like the *CSI* shows, she digs deep into the evidence in front of her to solve the mystery of a business problem.

The 'S' can stand for many things, but clients and colleagues agree it covers Simplicity, Systems and Solutions. And as for the BS, well Tamara cuts through it, pure and simple.

To connect with Tamara and find out how The BSi can help you get CLEAR on your BPS to build the simple, profitable business you love, please go to the website www.thebsi.com.au.

Testimonials

Tamara's professional advice and development of our policies, procedures and systems have proved extremely valuable in addressing our risk management and has provided a solid foundation on which our business can continue to grow. Under Tamara's guidance, we have also developed an organisational structure that specifically meets the requirements of our business.

Arthur Martin - Martin Design

I engaged Tamara to do an appraisal of my building company, Origin Builders. She came up with numerous ways we could operate more efficiently including better ways of communicating information from the office to the building sites, better ways of documenting our procedures with clients and contractors, and, most importantly, better ways of training my staff to run the business when I'm taking a break.

I was very impressed with the overall package put together for us and certainly feel I got value for money in what Tamara has done for us. I highly recommend Tamara to anyone looking to refine their business in order to provide better end results for their clients and be more competitive in the marketplace.

Ryan Brown - Origin Builders

Tamara Simon – what a presenter, the way she had everyone's attention for the whole presentation was outstanding. Tamara's experience and knowledge is extensive and her passion for the training industry is evident. I would not hesitate to recommend Tamara for our next presentation/conference.

Paul Baxter - Tranznet Conference and Baxter's Training Australia

I first met Tamara at a networking function, and on hearing of her area of expertise, I realised her services were the next essential step in the growth of my training company. Tamara has an amazing knack of cutting through the clutter in one's mind, tying together loose ends, and recommending and then implementing strategies and systems to get your business on track and moving forward with clarity. I would recommend her services to anyone needing structure and moving forward in their business.

Terri M Cooper - Real Estate Mastery

I'm a personal stylist and solopreneur and I was having a brainstorming session with Tamara not long ago as we were talking about each other's business. I started to discuss some of the things that were holding me back in my business, and within a short period of time, Tamara had given me such incredible ideas, a whole new strategy and something that I put into place as soon as we finished the conversation.

Never before, even in coaching sessions and seminars, had such a couple of brilliant lightbulb ideas been presented to me as in that short conversation with Tamara. And they were easily implementable strategies.

She's the Ideas Specialist. They will be worth a substantial amount of business to me as I put them into place. They were simple and incredibly effective and I can't understand why I hadn't thought of it myself. But that's why it was so worthwhile talking to someone with Tamara's skill and objective point of view.

She's responsible for a major boost in my productivity and profitability. Thanks heaps.

Anne Noonan - Anne's What Not to Wear

BSI provides a unique service – quick starts to get across a brief quickly. The work is of a high quality. It's accurate, tailored and timely. Highly recommended.

Vivienne Anthon - Australian Institute of Management

There's an old saying: 'When the student is ready, the teacher will arrive.' With impressive qualifications in business and human resource management, coupled with an intimate understanding of the building design profession, Tamara Simon has the knowledge and experience to provide customised systems and procedures to enable your business to become more efficient and profitable.

Tamara offers coaching in any or all aspects of your business. Policy and planning, financial and human resource management, risk management, document templates, workshops and in-house training are just a few of the areas of expertise offered.

The teacher has arrived; is the student ready? I commend to you Tamara Simon.

Greg Pershouse (Past President) - Building Designers' Association of Queensland and Northern Territory (BDAQ) and Greg Pershouse and Associates

Thanks for the great presentation at the Westside Business Women's breakfast meeting. What a breath of fresh air plus a down to earth manner of communicating methods and strategies about making things a whole lot easier working in business. Your topic 'Who is really running your business' made me stop, stand back and look at what I was doing. I get so busy and find I just keep doing what I've always done.

On my way back to work, my mind was racing with all the different methods that I could implement. Yes, it was time to make a few changes! WOW, where do I start? Give myself time out to work on the business, just have a coffee with a friend or to introduce a file system for my daily tasks? I'm looking at everything with new eyes and becoming more organised. Thank you Tamara.

Glenda Haig - Kids Under Cover and President Westside Business Women

Tamara utilises her vast experience to guide business owners on how to create more value in their business. She also helps them create the systems needed to ensure the business runs smoothly and efficiently.

Heather Boon - Maximum Results

I thank you for coaching me and my staff, working with us to not only help capture our knowledge but supporting us through the change management process which comes about by implementing systems.

Albert Daher - AAD Design

Thank you Tamara for helping me do the things I am hopeless at! Flowcharts, editing and all of the aspects of business that seem hard you made easy. I appreciate the speed at which you work and your efficiency.

Ingrid Dimock - City Chicks

Tamara Simon came out to my office to conduct a systems consultation. Whilst I already had a lot of processes in place, I felt overwhelmed by my office space and I didn't know how to improve its efficiency. Tamara helped me apply my business model to my physical space in a very simple and easy to understand manner. She prepared a written report that was easy to understand. As a result of the consultation, my office has now been reorganised in a more logical manner which has saved me around five hours each week. This gives me the ability to bill an additional $1,250 per week without working any longer. In this economic climate when businesses are searching for ways to improve their efficiency, Tamara can help improve the bottom line for businesses!

Maria Anderson - Sustainable Marketing Services Australia

Tamara has been able to implement a complete reversal in management philosophy, from a dictatorship style of management to an inclusive and democratic approach. This has been both at an operational level with staff and the organisation's management committee.

The organisation has achieved great success under Tamara's direction. This has been through the development of clear and concise marketing material to assist industry participation in accredited training; and rebuilding relationships with all of the abovementioned stakeholders which have been mended over time.

Grahame Henderson - Forest Industries ITAB

The time and effort you spent preparing and presenting training and information sessions for the graduates is sincerely appreciated. Your efforts were recognised in the positive ratings and comments received from the attendees.

Val Manera - Queensland Audit Office

Dementia Australia

My wonderful grandmother, a beautifully intelligent and fascinating lady, was taken from us too early because of this horrific disease. With your help, $2 from every book sold will be donated to Dementia Australia. Thank you very much and I pray we find a cure very soon.

Tamara

dementia australia™
research foundation

DEMENTIA AUSTRALIA
dementia.org.au

Dementia Australia represents more than 342,800 Australians living with dementia and the estimated 1.2 million Australians involved in their care, and acts as an advocate as well as providing support services, education and information.

WHAT IS DEMENTIA?
Dementia describes a collection of symptoms that are caused by disorders affecting the brain. It is not one specific disease. Dementia affects thinking, behaviour and the ability to perform everyday tasks. Brain function is affected enough to interfere with a person's normal social or working life.

WHO GETS DEMENTIA?
Most people with dementia are older, but it's important to remember that not all older people get dementia. It is not a normal part of ageing. Dementia can happen to anybody, but it's more common after the age of 65 years, even though people in their 40s and 50s can also have dementia.

WHAT CAUSES DEMENTIA?
There are many different forms of dementia, and each has its own causes. The most common types of dementia are Alzheimer's disease, Vascular dementia, Parkinson's disease, Dementia with Lewy bodies, Front-Temporal Lobar Degeneration (FTLD), Huntington's disease, Alcohol related dementia (Korsakoff''s syndrome) and Creutzfeldt-Jacob disease.

BSÎ

BUSINESS SCENE
INVESTIGATION®

Simplify Your Business

(+61) 438 262 727
INFO@THEBSI.COM.AU
WWW.THEBSI.COM.AU

TAMARA SIMON IS THE SIMPLE SOLUTIONS SPECIALIST.

Known as The BSi, she is all about solving Small Business problems with Simple Solutions.

As a Speaker, Author and Troubleshooter, Tamara helps Reluctant Business Owners build their Business, People and Systems (BPS) Roadmap for a simple profitable business they love. Tamara works with Business Owners who fundamentally want something in their business to change and value an external perspective to achieve this. These business owners generally:

- Know something's wrong in their business but aren't sure what it is
- Know what's wrong in their business but aren't sure how to fix it
- Want to grow or improve their business but aren't sure where to start or if their business is ready for this next step.

When Tamara talks to Business Owners, there are usually three comments she hears:

- *My turnover's great but there's little or no profit or money in the bank.*
- *I'm spending all my time dealing with staff – Ahh! I thought they were supposed to help me.*
- *Why do I have to keep fixing mistakes or putting out fires? Why can't everyone just do what they're supposed to do and do it correctly?*

Working with Tamara delivers you a clear, simple to execute strategy on how to transition your business to where you ultimately want it to be. You can have as much or as little support as you want; but in the end, your business will change for the better and the biggest problems you are experiencing will have simple solutions that <u>actually</u> work.

If this sounds like something you would like and something your business needs, Tamara would love the opportunity to have a one-on-one strategy chat with you. Take a look at her offer on the next page which is her thank you gift to her readers.

Please go to her website to connect with her on social media, send her an email or give her a call to find out how you can start re-building your business so it becomes simple, profitable and one you love.

www.ingramcontent.com/pod-product-compliance
Lightning Source LLC
Chambersburg PA
CBHW060238220326
41598CB00027B/3973